ROUTLEDGE LIBRARY EDITIONS:
ENERGY ECONOMICS

Volume 2

COAL ON THE SWITCHBACK

T0384425

COAL ON THE SWITCHBACK
The Coal Industry Since Nationalisation

ISRAEL BERKOVITCH

Routledge
Taylor & Francis Group

LONDON AND NEW YORK

First published in 1977 by George Allen & Unwin Ltd

This edition first published in 2018
by Routledge
2 Park Square, Milton Park, Abingdon, Oxon OX14 4RN

and by Routledge
711 Third Avenue, New York, NY 10017

Routledge is an imprint of the Taylor & Francis Group, an informa business

© 1977 George Allen & Unwin (Publishers) Ltd

All rights reserved. No part of this book may be reprinted or reproduced or utilised in any form or by any electronic, mechanical, or other means, now known or hereafter invented, including photocopying and recording, or in any information storage or retrieval system, without permission in writing from the publishers.

Trademark notice: Product or corporate names may be trademarks or registered trademarks, and are used only for identification and explanation without intent to infringe.

British Library Cataloguing in Publication Data
A catalogue record for this book is available from the British Library

ISBN: 978-1-138-10476-1 (Set)
ISBN: 978-1-315-14526-6 (Set) (ebk)
ISBN: 978-1-138-30398-0 (Volume 2) (hbk)
ISBN: 978-1-138-30401-7 (Volume 2) (pbk)
ISBN: 978-0-203-73050-8 (Volume 2) (ebk)

Publisher's Note
The publisher has gone to great lengths to ensure the quality of this reprint but points out that some imperfections in the original copies may be apparent.

Disclaimer
The publisher has made every effort to trace copyright holders and would welcome correspondence from those they have been unable to trace.

Coal on the Switchback

The Coal Industry since Nationalisation

Israel Berkovitch

With a foreword by Sir Derek Ezra

London
GEORGE ALLEN & UNWIN LTD
Ruskin House   Museum Street

First published in 1977

This book is copyright under the Berne Convention.
All rights are reserved. Apart from any fair dealing for
the purpose of private study, research, criticism or
review, as permitted under the Copyright Act, 1956,
no part of this publication may be reproduced, stored in
a retrieval system, or transmitted, in any form or by
any means, electronic, electrical, chemical, mechanical,
optical, photocopying, recording or otherwise, without
the prior permission of the copyright owner. Enquiries
should be addressed to the publishers.

© George Allen & Unwin (Publishers) Ltd, 1977

ISBN 0 04 622002 X hardback
     0 04 622003 8 paperback

Printed in Great Britain
in 11 on 12 point Baskerville
by Biddles Ltd, Guildford, Surrey

to my parents
to my wife and my daughter Anna who stood up to the domestic stresses
to the miners who provide so much of the fuel for the country – and the substance for my story

but without blaming any of them for the results.

Acknowledgements

In writing this history I have had extensive co-operation and support from the National Coal Board – notably from Mr Geoffrey Kirk, Director of Public Relations, Mr Philip Toms, of the Library, Mr Peter Heap, Senior Press Officer, Mr Bert Henry, Cuttings Library, and others. At the publishers I wish to acknowledge friendly co-operation and helpful suggestions. To all of them I am very grateful.

I must also express my appreciation for helpful, enlightening discussions with Dr E. Schumacher, Mr J. Gormley, Sir Richard Marsh and Mr Roy Mason, MP.

Foreword

by Sir Derek Ezra, chairman, National Coal Board

Everything that has happened since the events described in Dr Berkovitch's book has abundantly confirmed that no industrialised nation can afford to depend too heavily on imports of the energy that it must have. Oil is subject to political uncertainties. Its price has been pushed up so far and so rapidly that the big consuming nations are involved in a continuing and exhausting struggle to overcome the effects on their economies.

Even the United States, despite the underlying dynamism of its industries and the comparative richness of its natural resources, has not solved the problem as the exceptionally severe winter of 1976–7 showed. Energy policy remains one of the most urgent and difficult problems facing the American Administration.

The countries with the more stable economies and the stronger political influence in the future will be those who can supply all their own energy needs or whose imports are only a small proportion of the total.

Britain certainly has the potential quite quickly to become a member of that fortunate group. Oil and gas from the North Sea are coming ashore in substantial quantities and, together with coal, will soon be capable of meeting all the inland demand, at least well into the 1990s.

But coal is the only fossil fuel with long-term reserves and it will increasingly be used for more sophisticated purposes, supplementing oil as a source of chemicals and other materials for industry – and, indeed, for transport.

It should be possible, too, for Britain to become a net exporter of energy: such an achievement would transform our entire balance of payments.

The British coal industry is well placed to make its full contribution to this restoration of national prosperity. We have begun to search for fresh reserves and have had remarkable success. In fact we are now proving the existence of new coal measures at a rate four times as fast as the country is using them up. Already we know we can go on supplying the country's present needs for coal for about the next 300 years.

The Government have readily accepted the importance of developing this vast source of national wealth and are backing our investment programme with a substantial share of the capital resources that are available to them. Some existing pits have the reserves to justify major capital schemes and they show a very low cost per ton of additional annual capacity. In the case of new sites, the figure is usually a little higher but it is still an extremely attractive investment when compared to the alternative ways of creating new energy capacity.

The years Dr Berkovitch records were a stern test of the British coal industry's ability to survive as a viable entity. It emerged in a much contracted form (due to Government policies which were then pursued) but with undiminished credibility as a major supplier of the nation's energy in the circumstances that now exist.

During the late 1960s we at the Coal Board never wavered in our belief in the future of our industry, though, as Dr Berkovitch shows, it was often a somewhat lonely time for us. But the experiences we went through then are one of the sources of the zest with which we are now planning for expansion.

Contents

Illustrations

Tables

CHAPTER 1

The fuel picture

Energy is eternal delight
      'The marriage of heaven and hell' by William Blake

Animal and human muscles were for many centuries man's only source of power, while burning wood supplied heat for his comfort and cooking. In various parts of the world this was followed by a phase of burning dung as fuel – and over large areas these two natural products are still the main combustibles today. In Britain, coal has been scratched from the surface of the earth or from not very far below the surface, some say, for thousands of years. But particularly from the sixteenth century onward winning coal has become an ever more organised activity involving ever deeper burrowing into the bowels of the earth. By the early part of this century, the coal industry was in a dominating position in the economy. The centres of industry came to be built on the coalfields. Development reached its zenith in 1913 when 287 million tons of coal were produced in Britain and 94 million of them exported (including coal supplied to sea-going ships). At that time, Britain met almost 10 per cent of the demand for coal in the rest of the world. But in the general depression from the mid-twenties to the end of the thirties the industry was very severely affected. Output and exports fluctuated but generally fell and the share of the world's coal demand was also greatly reduced. An omen for the future was the increasing use of oil fuel by shipping in the period between the wars so that by 1935 only about half of the world's tonnage was fired by coal; for Britain this was reflected in a fall in the tonnage supplied for foreign bunkers from 21 million tons in that magic year 1913 to $13\frac{1}{2}$ million in 1935.

During the Second World War output declined, manpower fell; the Annual Report of the National Coal Board (NCB) for 1947 described many of the pits it had taken over as being 'in poor shape' and some as being 'in a pitiable condition'. Nevertheless, output was increased by a combination of short-term and long-term measures. But in 1957/58 a fresh turning-point was reached; coal stocks sharply increased and oil encroached with increasing success on the markets for coal. During the 1960s the gas and transport markets for coal virtually disappeared, while both domestic and industrial consumption were sharply cut. In 1950 coal had accounted for 90 per cent of the total energy in the country but its share had been halved by 1971. The industry was steadily, systematically run down. And while there had been about 140 closures of pits in the first decade after nationalisation during the expansion phase, these were mainly the result of exhaustion of reserves. The later waves of closures were largely due to their product being unable to compete with oil. Though leading figures in the coal industry campaigned vigorously against these closures, urging various forms of government support for coal, drawing attention to the dangers to national security in this heavy dependency on an imported fuel from a politically unstable part of the world, governments continued to operate policies intended to run down the industry in Britain (and in Western Europe), as discussed later.

As late as 1971 emphasis was still being placed on a 'cheap fuel policy' – meaning, in practice, continuing the switch away from coal. For example, the Coal Industry Act of 1971, providing for part of the social costs of closure to be met from Exchequer grants, was taken as an indication that the (Conservative) government did not anticipate any increase in the demand for coal, but by the end of 1972 the government was singing a very different tune. Mr Tom Boardman, Minister for Industry, introduced what became the Coal Industry Act 1973 – giving several forms of support to coal – by explaining that its object was to give the industry the opportunity to re-establish its financial viability, so that it could provide a secure and competitively-priced primary fuel, making its full contribution to the growing energy demand both within the

UK and overseas. Demand had fallen, he added, and the government had examined the alternative of letting the industry find its own level without any more aid than was provided in existing legislation. This course was rejected on social grounds and because it would have created an unacceptable danger to the security of the country's energy supplies.

Wise words spoken some ten years too late! For pits cannot be opened and shut like a tap, or even like a carefully cocooned factory; when they are shut down their skilled staffs are dispersed, the pits flood and choke up by underground movements. Britain was by then well and truly enmeshed in the potentially dangerous situation, at the mercy of the oil suppliers for quantities and prices. The situation was to lead to grave anxiety over supplies late in 1973 as the Arabs, after their attack on Israel, began to wield their oil weapon, and to an appalling burden subsequently on the balance of payments with no promise of relief until North Sea oil and increased coal supplies began to come through. But at least after the fivefold increase in oil prices by the Organisation of Petroleum Exporting Countries (OPEC) led by the Arabs, which resulted in this burden, the attractions of coal to earlier official and industrial sceptics became more clearly evident. One of the strangest indications of this was the choice of a coal industry float escorted by miners to lead the industrial section in the Lord Mayor of London's 1974 procession. As high as a double-decker bus, the float was explicitly intended to symbolise the importance of coal for Britain's future.

A more formal indication was the announcement by the Labour government which came into power in 1974 of a 'commitment' to the success of the industry – a complete reversal of its policy during the period 1964–70 – in addition to major efforts to speed the supply of oil from the North Sea. On the government's behalf, Mr Eric Varley, Secretary of State for Energy, promised backing for the heavy investment programme to secure 42 million tons per annum of extra coal capacity by 1985, support for more research into new uses for coal, but also the long overdue humane feature of early compensation to pneumoconiosis sufferers and an improved

pension scheme for mineworkers. Yet the effects of the earlier
rundown proved so difficult to reverse that when this latest
switch of demand came, the coal industry was unable to meet
it immediately – the difficulties being aggravated but not
basically caused by the coal strikes, which were themselves
a consequence of the declining position of the miners largely
due to the rundown of the industry. There were imports of
coal in 1971, 1972, 1973 and 1974. (For example, about $3\frac{1}{2}$
million tons were imported in 1974.)

So coal has truly been on a switchback of rising and falling
fortunes many times repeated. It is the aim of this book to
look more particularly at its history in Britain since nationalisation but to set it in perspective by looking briefly at its
earlier history; furthermore, since the market for fuel is international, the story will also look at world trends and their
impact on the main subject.

MODERN MAN NEEDS FUEL

To drive his machines, man needs fuel. And it is widely
understood that standards of living are linked with the power
available per head of the population so that the energy consumption is related to the Gross National Product (GNP).
However, detailed examination of these concepts shows many
complications and the amount of energy needed to produce
$1 of GNP varies widely throughout the world. There are
excellent discussions of these themes in such books as *Energy
in the World Economy* by Joel Darmstadter (Resources for
the Future, 1971) and *World Markets of Tomorrow* by
Fremont Felix (Harper and Row, 1972). Today, in the industrialised parts of the world it is customary to query not only
the relationship between energy consumption per head and
GNP or average income but also whether the latter criteria
measure living standards – or, more fundamentally, human
happiness. Without delving too far into these issues, we can
simply observe that there is a connection between economic
development and increasing use of fuel. In practice, modern
industrial production and social amenities depend on the
availability of sources of energy, and any threat to the supplies

causes disruption to our way of life, irrespective of social or philosophical criticisms of its character. What, then, have been the trends in the use of energy and how have they been met?

The most striking feature has been that coal has lost ground throughout the world in recent years while oil and natural gas have greatly increased their shares of the energy market. Until 1974 world energy consumption grew in the period after the Second World War at generally increasing rates; before the oil crises the growth rate was around $5\frac{1}{2}$ per cent each year. This meant that energy consumption per head was increasing at about $3\frac{1}{2}$ per cent, adding to the increase resulting from population growth of 2 per cent. Within this overall effect there were marked regional differences. The USA uses much more energy per annum than any other country and the consumption per head per annum in the USA and Canada is double that in Western Europe (though this difference is tending to narrow) and up to forty times the corresponding figures for Africa and the developing parts of Asia. The USA emerged as a large-scale importer of foreign oil, likely to increase its dependence on this source in the future; the US government has consequently begun to take urgent measures to control and ultimately, it hopes, to reverse this trend, achieving energy self-sufficiency by 1985 by a programme understandably known as Project Independence.

The shares of world energy consumption increased – owing to relatively faster growth in the use of energy per head of population – in the Soviet Union, Eastern Europe, Western Europe, Japan especially but also other parts of Asia, Canada and elsewhere, corresponding to a decreasing share of usage by the USA which still, because of its much higher starting-point, remained by far the biggest user of energy. The extent to which coal met these growing requirements fell as a share of the total in all areas, while natural gas tended to gain in its share similarly consistently, and so did oil except in Latin America. In most parts of the world, absolute levels of coal production declined, except in the USA, USSR, China and Poland, and capacity was reduced by closing pits and reducing investment in the industry. The rundown was exceptionally rapid in Western Europe in the EEC where coal – at an earlier stage the only industrial fuel of its constituent nations – contributed less than a quarter of its primary energy needs in 1973 and the Community became overwhelmingly dependent on oil to the extent of over 61 per cent. Natural gas was by then the source of over a tenth of its primary energy. Japan, with its exceptional rate of economic growth, developed an even more severe dependence on imported oil and put heavy investments into Abu Dhabi and South East Asia, particularly into Indonesia, to try to protect its position as well as conducting exploration in some twenty-five countries for fresh sources of the precious fluid. Where was all this oil to come from? In 1973 Darmstadter quoted figures shown here in Table 1 as 'currently published proved reserves figures for the potential net exporting regions of the world (excluding, that is, the United States, Western Europe and the Communist countries)'.

Table 1   *Published proved oil reserves for potential net exporting regions (Darmstadter)*

	billion barrels
Middle East: Saudi Arabia	183
Middle East: Other	172
North Africa	83
All other	81
TOTAL	519

(And, incidentally, even if North Sea oil makes Britain an exporter, the quantities are too small to influence this pattern.)

EARLIER FORECASTS

Was it totally unexpected to discover that the industrial nations of the world had delivered themselves into the hands of the Arabs, and notably of Saudi Arabia, by their fuel policies over the previous fifteen years or so? The reason for the shift, of course, had been mainly that oil was cheaper on a unit energy basis and had a higher calorific value per unit weight. For domestic use the fluid fuels are much more convenient in use, though this is less true for industrial/commercial application or in power stations where appropriate handling equipment enables coal to be handled and fed to the furnaces conveniently. So industrialists and those responsible for generating electricity were influenced largely by the immediate issue of relative price per unit of energy. But governments and policy-makers should have had a wider-ranging vision. Is this simply a matter of being wise after the event? Here are some quotations from a pamphlet entitled *Meeting Europe's Energy Requirements* published in 1963 by the West European Coal Producers and the National Coal Board. This necessarily started from a review of the world energy market before turning to the implications for Europe. Writing at a time of cheap oil and fuel 'surplus' the authors concluded:

> An objective view of the world market for energy, then, leads decisively to this conclusion: **if the expansion of the world economy continues, a fuel shortage 10 to 20 years from now is more likely than a surplus.**

(The heavy type is used in the original.) Suppose, then, that official policy-makers accepted this as a real possibility but thought in terms of temporary reductions in coal capacity while there was a glut. The answer was explicit:

> If a coal industry is forced into rapid contraction, coal reserves equal to many years or even decades of normal output may be irretrievably lost. These reserves cannot be recovered except in exceptional cases or at exorbitant cost. It follows that an indefensible waste of natural resources is incurred when a coal industry is forced to adjust its size to short-lived falls in demand, such as the one currently caused by the world glut of oil and gas. No less real is the sociological fact that . . . it is impossible to re-create a mining labour force at short notice, no matter how urgent the need for coal.

The likely consequences of the then current trends were equally clearly spelt out :

> If by 1975 Europe's coal output were to be cut down to 300 million tons, Europe would be compelled to import no less than 50 per cent of her energy needs . . . Excessive reliance on fuel imports would expose Europe not only to the inevitable increases of prices on the world fuel market, but also to substantial price fluctuations which are disturbing to the whole economy. Even a policy of holding large fuel stocks, which would be costly, would afford little security.
>
> There is, finally, the balance of payments problem, which deserves attention.

All this shows just how unforeseeable was our present plight. But, the critic might argue – and I have met complacent senior officials at the Department of Energy who do – 'what would be the cost of alternative policies than the one actually adopted, of slashing the coal industry?' Both this pamphlet and other papers written personally by Dr E. F. Schumacher examined such costs in relation to the output of the West European economy that was thus being put at risk (as summarised below) and in relation to military expenditure, a very relevant comparison since national security was involved for all the countries due to become heavy oil importers to meet the needs of industry *and indeed of the military themselves.* The main proposal that the coal advocates were combating was that of cutting coal output to 300 million tons per year by 1975 (it was in fact down to 227 by 1973); their own scheme was based on a level of 500 million tons. Quoting from the arguments of those most in favour of a cheap fuel policy that the decline would be at a rate of 20 million tons of output a year, the coal producers allowed for a price differential that might go up to $3 a ton and concluded that if support of some kind were needed it would amount to the equivalent of one-tenth of 1 per cent of the aggregated national products overall by the end of the ten-year period, allowing for the expected rise in the national products of the countries concerned. Some individual producers would be seriously affected and these would need special government measures of support. This interference with normal free market operation, they concluded, was essential since

> the future availability of European hard coal will become a matter of decisive importance for the safety and health of the European economy, and the real task of a fuel policy for Western Europe is to enable the indigenous fuel suppliers to meet their future obligations. . . . Having set out these issues as we see them, we submit them to our respective governments, with whom rests the final responsibility for ensuring the security of fuel supplies for the economy of Western Europe.

The general reaction to this and further campaigning by coal producers, such as Lord Robens in the UK, was that it constituted special pleading by a sectional interest promoting its own case. Sir Frederick Catherwood, Director-General of the National Economic Development Office during this period, admitted in 1974, for example, that his own reactions had been along these lines but that he had later appreciated the validity of the case for maintaining the size of the coal industry in the national interest, even at some cost to the rest of the economy. Others, less honest, admitted nothing and when the crunch came were more likely to blame the miners.

In the early years after the Second World War, nuclear energy was thought to have not only glamour but also early potential. Its advocates, of course, had to fight off the uneasiness of popular reaction resulting from the horrifying accounts of the consequences of its use in war against the Japanese and the fact that its early development was an off-shoot of continuing bomb-making. Yet there was also popular appeal in the concept of this form of turning swords into ploughshares; the Americans even called their programme for peaceful uses of atomic energy by the evocative name 'Plowshare'. And public interest was stimulated by accounts of the large amounts of energy theoretically available from small amounts of fissile fuel so that even the most scientifically-philistine of arts men was able to quote the Einstein formula $E = Mc^2$ for the equivalence of mass and energy (M being the mass in grams, c the velocity of light in cm per sec giving E the energy in ergs).

The first pile began to work in 1942. The USA spent many thousands of millions of dollars on atomic energy programmes in the immediate post-war period, and even Britain spent £100 million between 1946 and 1951. But reports to the Sixth World Power Conference in 1962 indicated that the total power to be expected from plans for civil nuclear energy would provide less than 1 per cent of world requirements. In practice, by 1972, the proportion was estimated as 0·8 per cent. And, though Britain was the first country to generate electricity from a nuclear station on an industrial scale, in 1956 – the Russians had a small-scale nuclear reactor designed primarily for producing electrical power working in 1954 – its nuclear programme has faced delays due to technical difficulties which have held back development. Over the period 1969–1974, for example, the contribution of nuclear electricity to Britain's energy usage has stayed more or less steady at the equivalent of about 10 million tons of coal per year. And it is only in the last few years that the power generated by these plants has been surpassed by that of the rest of the world combined. So, though current plans continue to assume that nuclear power will form an increasing component of the provision of energy in the future, it has played little part so far. The dazzling vision of untold wealth of energy from small amounts of fuel was soon obscured by difficulties of corrosion, premature wear and other troubles linked with fears about safety, resulting in both delays and heavier costs of construction. Furthermore, it faces a well-informed hostile 'lobby' of critics concerned at its production of long-lived radioactive wastes.

Hydroelectric schemes provide most of the electricity for some few countries such as Norway, Sweden, Switzerland and Uganda – and may sometimes be linked with multi-purpose projects such as providing irrigation, as in India, Pakistan and Egypt. Yet on a world scale this source is reckoned to provide only about 6 per cent of the energy, even though this corresponds to about a third of the world's electricity. For Britain this is a very minor supplier yielding a fraction of 1 per cent of total needs.

In various places, making contributions to local needs, solar energy, geothermal sources (from eruptions at the surface or by drilling), tidal and wind power have all been used. Whatever their prospects for the future, they have as yet made little impact on world needs for industrial, transport and domestic power.

RESERVES

Since this rapid review shows that man is dependent on fossil fuels – deposits within the earth's crust of combustible materials formed over long periods of time – for most of his sources of energy, the remaining essential is to check the reserves of these fuels. Briefly, the answer from geological surveying and estimating is that it is coal that has by far the largest reserves. This apparently simple conclusion, however, covers a multitude of complications concerned with both the method of estimating and the accessibility of these natural stores. In respect of estimating, the problem is vastly different from that of, say, taking stock of defined, accessible materials in a factory. In assessing reserves physical, geological, technological and economic factors have all to be taken into account. Gross reserves of coal estimated from borings and underground sampling will include a large proportion that is unworkable owing to severe geological disturbance, disturbance by earlier workings, risk of flooding, risk of disturbing the surface, or other factors affecting the possibility of economic working.

At a Royal Society meeting in 1973, Mr D. C. Ion of the World Energy Conference 1974 Resources Survey drew attention to the fact that a great diversity of people collect these reserves data and estimates are then amended by the opinions of those who are collecting them. Consequently, it became necessary to agree on definitions for the survey which represented a compromise between different reserves concepts and tended to involve changes from earlier definitions.

In respect of coal, for example, emphasis is now placed on what can be recovered under current operating and economic conditions; these vary from place to place and are influenced

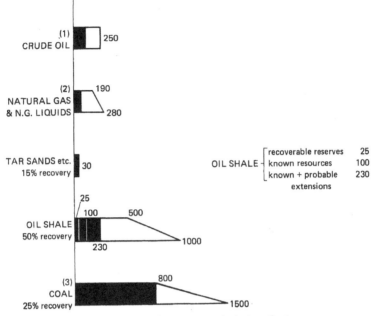

Fig. 1 World Recoverable Hydrocarbon Reserves. (in Gt. i.e. 10ᵃ tonnes oil equivalent). Source: Programmes Analysis Unit, Harwell (1974).

by local environmental interest, such as strong objections to a coal of high sulphur content, which should therefore be excluded (presumably unless it can be burned under acceptable conditions, which is now possible). For oil reserves the definition was that the quantities to be returned were those remaining in the ground which information indicates with reasonable certainty to be recoverable based on the present state of technology and under existing economic conditions. Similar definitions, heavily weighted towards the practical possibilities of recovery, were laid down for natural gas (associated or not associated with oil), bituminous sands and oil shales, hydraulic energy, nuclear energy and the renewable sources such as solar and tidal energy.

The importance of these attempts at standardisation can be indicated by the range of values quoted in the report of the

Institute of Fuel, *Energy for the Future,* published in 1973. In a table giving what are described as 'present known' world energy reserves, the lowest estimate for coal is quoted as equivalent to 30 years' life at the rate of use in 1971, soaring to 190 years' life for the highest estimate. For completeness it should be added that the report gives further estimates for potential future reserves considered to be recoverable allowing for improvements in the technology of extraction and price rises. In these terms the expected life is increased; at future consumption rates the lowest estimate becomes 150 and the highest 250 years.

Probably the most authoritative figures, bringing together the work of foremost researchers throughout the world, are those of the Survey of Energy Resources 1974 prepared for the World Energy Conference of that year. According to these, almost half of the total energy content in the recoverable quantities of measured reserves of all fossil fuels is contained in the solid ones, 12 per cent in crude oil and about half that amount in natural gas. The quantities mentioned here are considered well-defined. The balance of about a third of all these reserves is in oil shales and bituminous sands, but these estimates are considered far less reliable. Total quantities of fossil fuels are thought to be about twenty times the quantity of those now recoverable. These reserves of coal are held to be more than adequate to meet any likely level of future demand on a world scale, though other features may limit the rate at which they can be tapped. For Britain, Mr G. Armstrong, at that time the Chief Geologist of the NCB, gave a figure in 1970 which corresponded with a life of possibly sixty years, but since then vast new reserves have been proved in thick seams in the Selby area of Yorkshire, in Staffordshire and in the Notts coalfield. Britain's coal reserves are puny on the world scale, and the main bulk of all solid fuels is in the USA, USSR, and China, though there are also large amounts in Europe, Canada, Australia, India and South Africa.

For oil and gas, figures given above indicate that the reserves are much more limited and that those of oil are heavily concentrated in the area surrounding the Persian Gulf (which also has about a fifth of the natural gas). Cynics tend to reassure themselves with the thought that for many decades there has always been thirty years reserve of oil, that there have perennially been forecasters of doom, and that fresh deposits nevertheless continue to be found. Yet there is now a general impression that this process is nearing its end. The Institute of Fuel, drawing on many expert sources, concluded that the potential future recoverable reserves ranged between thirty years of life on a world scale as the lowest estimate and only forty as the highest, for oil, with very similar ranges for gas. Production outside the communist world was assessed in 1973 as likely to reach a peak during the 1980s, and even the big price increases are expected to delay this only by a decade or so. Because of this, the UK Programmes Analysis Unit sees the need for a massive increase in world coal production but adds that even this will be insufficient to counterbalance the eventual decline in natural oil and gas production, so that it postulates the manufacture of hydrogen and methane fuel gases using nuclear energy in the next few decades. The US government has accepted a very similar analysis of expected decline and has set up a large programme for developing synthetic fuels from coal. Expenditure on this work represents a large fraction of the total of its National Energy Program. The Program is officially declared to be directed 'to first supplement and then replace oil and natural gas on a massive scale' and to have been given top priority because of its importance in alleviating the energy crisis in both the short and the midterm period.

Nuclear power might seem to be immune from anxieties about reserves since its basis is the conversion of small amounts of matter into vast quantities of energy. Yet, in practice, the efficiency of generating electricity by this means combined with the size of the programmes based on this source of energy for the future led the Institute of Fuel to refer to the problem of depletion of uranium resources – and this despite the fact that there have been intensive searches for uranium and also some success in finding thorium while exploring for minerals of various metals. The magic key due to open the door to boundless energy from fission is seen in the form of the breeder reactor – which breeds further fissionable fuel from uranium or thorium during the process of generating electricity – but for several reasons 'more problems remain to be solved with breeders than thermal reactors' and their commercial use taking over a large part of the energy load is not an early prospect.

For completeness, we should also refer to the oil shales and bituminous sands, noted earlier as possibly accounting for about a third of all world reserves of fossil fuels. Almost all these resources are in North America (both in the USA and Canada), with much smaller amounts in the USSR, China, Zaire, Italy and Sweden. They have been little used in the past but are now being actively reconsidered, in the face of very intense opposition from environmentalists who fear des-poliation of the countryside both in the extraction and in the disposal of the residue after processing.

SUMMARY

We can therefore summarise the world fuel picture in these terms. In recent decades world energy consumption has increased at a compound rate of about $5\frac{1}{2}$ per cent per annum. In meeting this demand, coal has lost ground to oil and natural gas. A major consequence has been growing depen-dence on imported fuels – particularly oil from Arab countries – by all the industrialised countries, including the USA, until recently a fuel exporter. Yet coal has by far the greater reserves. For both these reasons, major efforts are now being made to regenerate the coal industry and to develop chemical processes for converting it into fluid fuels. Nuclear reactions may well in due course be a major source of energy but so far have contributed little and the problems of developing this source have proved far greater than were originally expected.

Renewable resources have been little applied, except for hydraulic power used to generate electricity which has been important for some countries with heavy rainfall and suitable physical features.

The USA, the Soviet Union and the countries of Eastern Europe have maintained large coal industries, but those of the EEC ran down coalmining capacity so that they became heavily dependent on oil imports. The EEC is now adopting a new energy policy to slow down the demand for oil, including the development of a more competitive coal industry and the importing of coal. Britain broadly followed world trends in the period after the Second World War, at first seeking to build up its coal industry, then systematically closing it down in pursuit of a cheap fuel policy, interfering little with the switch to cheaper oil.

What was the background to this policy? How do the chief actors now justify their parts in that drama that led the country close to the risk of economic strangulation? Both official and unofficial explanations of these central issues of policy will be treated and analysed in some detail in the later chapters of this book. By 1974, the newly arrived Labour government, after the reappraisals following the rapid five-fold increase in oil prices, expressed a commitment to building the coal industry. It also took major decisions on nuclear policy which, despite massive investment, was contributing only some 3 per cent to the primary energy input. And, of course, oil from the North Sea was expected to make Britain a net exporter of oil from about 1980, while further discoveries of gas promised a greater contribution of this fuel to future energy supplies. Repercussions of these new features form the theme of the concluding chapters.

SUGGESTED FURTHER READING

Pauline Gregg, *A Social and Economic History of Britain 1760 – 1965* (Harrap, 5th edition, 1965)

Joel Darmstadter, *Energy in the World Economy* (Resources for the Future, 1971)

Fremont Felix, *World Markets of Tomorrow* (Harper and Row, London 1972)

Energy in the 1980s (Royal Society, 1974)

Meeting Europe's Energy Requirements (Memorandum by the West European Coal Producers and the National Coal Board, 1963)

Energy Resources for Western Europe: Present Situation and Future Prospects (Association for Coal in Europe, 1971)

Energy Trends (Department of Energy, monthly)

Energy for the Future (Institute of Fuel, 1973)

CHAPTER 2

From scrabbling in the ground to exporting great treasure

Oh where are you going to all you great steamers
With England's own coal, up and down the salt seas
                    'Big Steamers' by Rudyard Kipling

Though there are interesting speculations on the theme of how far back, and in which countries, coal was first recognised as a combustible rock and scratched out of the ground for use as a fuel, all that is relevant here – in this potted preamble to the story of the most recent phases of the industry – is to note that the fuel was little used before the sixteenth century. And though the men, women and small children who hewed and extracted it were treated with contempt by the cleaner-handed members of society, coal was very largely the base of the growth of the industry and commerce that established British commercial supremacy before the Industrial Revolution. Professor J. U. Nef, 'with considerable hesitation', because he had to estimate from very incomplete and fragmentary sources, suggests that the growth of the coal industry may be indicated by the figures shown in Table 2. In this table, the figures for the Midlands include output from Yorkshire, Lancashire, Cheshire, Derbyshire, Shropshire, Staffordshire, Nottinghamshire, Warwickshire, Leicestershire and Worcestershire, and of course the figures for the earlier decades are the less reliable.

Nef also reviews alternative theories concerning the rapid transformation of Great Britain during the period 1550–1700.

Giving due weight to such factors as her keeping aloof from continental quarrels, permitting the passage of goods from one part to another without the payment of heavy tolls (as against the high tariffs payable on the Continent), and gaining control over a vast and wealthy colonial empire, he nevertheless concludes : 'What has not been recognised is that commercial

Table 2   *Estimated annual production of the principal mining districts (in tons)*

Coalfield	1551–60	1681–90	1781–90	1901–10
Durham and				
Northumberland	65,000	1,225,000	3,000,000	50,000,000
Scotland	40,000	475,000	1,600,000	37,000,000
Wales	20,000	200,000	800,000	50,000,000
Midlands	65,000	850,000	4,000,000	100,180,000
Cumberland	6,000	100,000	500,000	2,120,000

supremacy was based to no small extent upon the growth of native industry, and that the growth both of industry and commerce was based to no small extent upon coal.' Britain throughout the Middle Ages was economically a backwater but rose during this period to 'a place in the front rank'.

The growth of coal-mining here during that time was unique : production in the rest of the world is estimated to have been only one-sixth of that of Britain, while Holland, one of her chief economic rivals, had no coal, and France, the other main rival, had very little. Furthermore, the coal industry promoted the growth of capitalistic forms of organisation since groups of miners in partnership found they were forced into dependence on traders; mining enterprises became larger and began to employ salaried officials and to show sharp cleavage between labour and the owners of capital. The repercussions of the developing demand for coal gave further stimulus to industrial and economic development. To move the increasing quantities over longer distances, wagonways were invented for movement over land and large ships for the sea traffic. Like the growth of the modern home-based oil industry, that of the coal industry of that time necessitated the construction or dredging of harbours, the deepening of rivers, and the setting up of coastal equipment.

Progress in many industries was also related to the expansion of the coal industry. Nef cites the manufacture of salt, glass, alum and certain branches of the metallurgical and shipbuilding industries increasingly carried on in establishments that were not within the ordinarily accepted meaning of the term 'domestic system'. The increasing deepening of mines also created needs which stimulated technology. The man credited by J. D. Bernal, author of *Science in History,* with the first success in designing and financing 'a workable fire-driven pump' was a Captain Savery of the Royal Engineers (he died in 1715) who called his patent application 'The Miner's Friend'; the engine was intended for draining mines. In due course it was superseded by a more practical one made in 1712 by Thomas Newcomen. Improved versions of steam-engines later provided power for a wide range of industries, spreading overseas and often set up by British engineers. But the original spur came from the mines. Professor E. J. Hobsbawm calls steam-engines 'the product of the mines'.

However, the 'base load' for coal was the domestic market in the cities and particularly in London. The combined effect was a demand for coal that exceeded a million tons a year during the seventeenth century, continuing to grow and becoming the first commodity used on this great scale. And though demand grew during the Industrial Revolution, when the pacemaker was cotton and its industrial development involved the inefficient burning of increasing amounts of coal, Hobsbawm states that as late as 1842 it was still the smoky fireplaces in Britain that consumed two-thirds of Britain's domestic coal supplies, which had risen by then to some 30 million tons, representing probably two-thirds of the entire output of the Western world.

HUMAN COSTS

What were the human costs of the rapid development of the coal industry? Historians of its earlier stages cite such features as ostracism of miners, deprivation of civil rights, and their treatment as primitive and uncouth creatures; it was of course a very dangerous occupation with relatively high risks of sudden death or appalling injury from explosions, falls of earth or uncontrollable inrush of water. To these were added humiliation and legal disabilities. An Act of 1697 is said to have conferred on coalmasters the right of apprehending vagabonds and their children without the need for trial in a court of law. At one stage in Scotland, mining was lifelong servitude – that is actual slavery – and as late as 1765 a claim was made by coalmasters in Northumberland and Durham to be empowered to tie miners to one enterprise as in Scotland. In 1699, seventeen convicts had their sentences remitted on condition that they bound themselves to work in the mines for five years, thus treating this occupation as equivalent to a prison sentence and further depressing the already low social status of the miners and their communities.

The coalmasters employed women and children in the pits until the Mines Act – introduced as the Mines Bill in 1842 – prohibited the work of women and girls and of boys under ten years old. It followed publication of the alarming findings of an official investigation. 'Not until the searchlight of a Government Commission lit the dark places of the mine in 1842,' wrote Pauline Gregg, 'was there revealed a true picture of the life going on beneath the soil of a country which was congratulating itself that its rising assets were being balanced by an equivalent growth of humanitarianism'. The Commissioners themselves noted that public attention had been given to conditions in mills and factories and to the distress of a large body of hand-loom weavers. But little was known of the condition of persons employed in mining. The resultant report remains a compulsively readable humane document. It was natural, the Commissioners conceded, that less should be known of work in the mines than of other 'descriptions of labour' of equal importance, because the operations were wholly removed from ordinary view, the places in which they were carried on were relatively inaccessible, and the operations themselves were peculiar. They therefore set out in great detail how they had conducted their investigation, explaining the care they had taken to ensure the correctness of the information gathered and to guard it from being of a partial and *ex-parte* character, so that they could exhibit a faithful picture of the physical and moral condition of the juvenile working population. What were their findings?

   In regard to coal mines

    1   That instances occur in which children are taken into these mines to work as early as four years of age, sometimes at five, and between five and six, not unfrequently between six and seven, and often from seven to eight, while from eight to nine is the ordinary age at which employment in these mines commences.

    3   That in several districts female children begin to work in these mines at the same early age as the males.

    7   That the nature of the employment which is assigned to the youngest children, generally that of 'trapping', requires that they should be in the pit as soon as the work of the day commences and . . . not leave the pit before the work of the day is at an end.

    8   That . . . as the Children . . . are commonly excluded from light and are always without companions, it would, were it not for the passing and repassing of the coal carriages, amount to solitary confinement of the worst order.

   13   That when the workpeople are in full employment, the regular hours of work for Children and Young Persons are rarely less than eleven; more often they are twelve; in some districts they are thirteen; and in one district they are generally fourteen and upwards.

Here and there, the Commissioners were able to draw attention to mitigating features. In many instances, they wrote, much that skill and capital could effect to render the place of work unoppressive, healthy and safe had been done. Yet they were forced to come back to noting that in a great many instances the condition in respect of both ventilation and drainage was 'lamentably defective'. They were also concerned with the demoralising effect of having both sexes working together nearly or completely naked. In general, younger children were roughly used by their older companions and in many mines the conduct of the adult colliers to the children and young people was harsh and cruel. The evidence included verbatim accounts such as this :

> In the very small collieries, . . . little children are sent into holes in the mines with baskets to get coals to bring to the foot of the shaft, and then drag them along on their hands and knees.

For Halifax, this was the description given :

> In this district the loaded corves drawn by the hurriers weigh from 2 to 5 cwt; these carriages are mounted upon four cast-iron wheels. . . . The Children have to drag these carriages through passages in some cases not more than from 16 to 20 inches in height . . . they buckle round their naked persons a broad leather strap, to which is attached in front a ring and about 4 feet of chain terminating in a hook. This illustration of the circumstances of this degrading labour is so much more forcible than any verbal description, that we must claim permission to subjoin it.

And the Commissioners reinforced the verbal description with these powerful sketches.

Accidents 'of a fearful nature' were found to be extremely

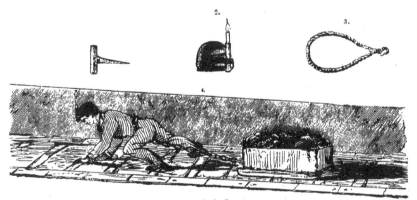

Fig. 2   A sketch from the First Report of the Commissioners on the Employment of Children in Coal Mines, 1842.

frequent, happening even in the sight of the Commissioners during their inspections of pits. Causes were listed as lack of supervision, neglect of machinery, overloading, ignoring the presence of gas, inadequate ventilation, relying on children for controlling air-doors. Let me conclude with just one further group of quotations from the conclusions which give the flavour of the pits towards the end of the great Industrial Revolution.

22   That there are many mines in which the most ordinary precautions to guard against accidents are neglected, and in which no money appears to be expended with a view to secure the safety, much less the comfort, of the workpeople.

26   That partly by the severity of the labour and the long hours of work, and partly through the unhealthy state of the place of work, this employment . . . deteriorates the physical constitution; in the thin seam mines, more especially, the limbs become crippled and the body distorted.

27   That by the same causes the seeds of painful and mortal diseases are very often sown in childhood and youth. . . .

The further fruits of this enquiry were gathered only after another eight years and several serious mining accidents. An additional Act extended the powers of inspectors, enabling them to report on the condition of mines and machinery. A clause along these lines in the earlier Bill had been removed by the House of Lords.

But, apart from the legal consequences, in many other ways, as one commentator observed :

These horrific working conditions left their mark : on the miner as a bitter folk memory and feeling of isolation from other industrial workers; on society as a mixture of guilt and fear of the miner as a separate species of worker. These attitudes survive throughout the industry's history, showing

themselves particularly starkly at the times of crisis inform-
ing all other considerations.

Within the pits themselves, despite some improvements in
conditions resulting from this lifting of the veil on the methods
of the coal-mining industry, the continuing increases in output
were bought at a price that included the blood of many
miners. Hobsbawm records that coal production rose from 49
million tons in 1850 to 147 million tons by 1880, but also
that about 1,000 miners a year were killed in accidents over
the period 1856 to 1886. The vast increase was evidently
achieved without any significant technical development, for
the number of miners also grew almost at the same rate as the
tonnage, to a total of half a million men around 1880.

PATTERN OF DECLINE

Led notably by a railway boom at home and abroad, the
economy, though it went through good years and bad, demanded ever greater quantities of coal, and the output figure
attained 225 million tons at the turn of the century. Yet other
countries, notably the USA, with 241 million tons, were
developing even faster. In the railway age Britain had led
and had set the standard for other countries. But during the
first decade of the twentieth century there developed what
Pauline Gregg calls a 'second Industrial Revolution' based on
the growth of steel, electric power and the internal combustion
engine, forming a parallel to the iron, coal and steam transport of the first one. In this, Britain was no longer the domi-
nant force. It was this period which saw the highest ever rate
of output of coal from British pits – 287 million tons in 1913,
of which 73 million were exported abroad and 21 million
supplied 'for the use of steamers engaged in the foreign trade',
as the old Department of Mines described it. Including the
coal equivalent of the coke and manufactured fuel, the grand
total shipped abroad amounted to over 98 million tons. These
dazzling attainments were never repeated. For the following
twenty-one – largely troubled – years, the Political and Economic Planning (PEP)* Report quoted from the Department
of Mines the information shown here in Table 3.

Table 3   *Output and consumption of coal 1913–34*

	1913	1920	1929	1930	1931	1932	1933	1934
Output of coal in United Kingdom	287·35	229·42	257·91	243·88	219·46	208·73	207·11	220·73
Total quantity of coal shipped abroad	98·34	43·68	82·15	75·10	61·65	57·15	56·68	57·09
Home consumption per head of population in cwt	89	85	78	75	69	67	66	71

*Political and Economic Planning (PEP) is an institute that is independent, non-party, not run for profit and recognised as an educational charity. Studies are made by qualified research staff with advisory groups of specialists. In the 1930s it defined itself as 'consisting of more than a hundred working members who are by vocation industrialists, distributors, officers of central and local government, university teachers and so forth, and who give part of their spare time to the use of their special training in fact-finding and in suggesting principles and possible advances over a wide range of social and economic activities'. At that time the group had issued some seventy broadsheets on a considerable variety of subjects and published full-scale reports on the cotton and iron and steel industries, housing and building, retirement pensions and continued education.

The decline in home *per capita* consumption, particularly in the last few years cited, was attributed in part to the effects of depression but also demonstrated the great economies made in the use of fuel, since the figure for the world boom year of 1929 (though it was a year of considerable industrial activity) remained well below that of 1913.

The period between the two world wars in Britain was generally one of decline characterised at times by great hardship and misery with continuing mass unemployment. The mild boom that followed the First World War slid into a general depression by mid-1920. There was some degree of recovery in 1922 to 1924 and, in the world as a whole, the following five years showed a marked improvement in trade. Shortly afterwards came the oft-analysed world crisis, and this included a time when the number of people unemployed in Britain approached three million. Recovery during the thirties was slow. For example, there were still 1·8 million unemployed in 1938. Exports fell and imports rose, and Pauline Gregg comments that the only important raw material in which Britain remained self-supporting was coal. Yet in this unhappy framework, how had it fared?

Coal, in fact, proved to be the industry that suffered most from the world depression and the decline in British exports. The details of this inter-war decline in export trade were documented in the PEP Report. Its analysis opens by noting that 'the coalfields of Britain are situated to the best possible advantage for export trade . . . the average length of haul for export coal being no more than 25 miles'. This distance compared with estimated averages of 50 miles for the Belgians, up to 70 for the French, over 100 for the Germans (though they have their internal waterways) and no less than 400 miles for the Poles. To rub in the message, the Report added that these natural advantages were so great that the British industry under conditions of free competition could land coal on the German North Sea coast or at the American North Atlantic ports rather more cheaply than supplies from the respective indigenous mines.

Despite this, there was only one good year for exports in this period. In 1923 exports to both France and Germany (two of the three pre-war principal markets) were exceptionally inflated, owing to the occupation of the Ruhr and domestic difficulties in France. Otherwise the export market fell, as broadly indicated in Table 2 above. The real turning-point was generally taken to be the long strike in 1926 which followed the Samuel Commission's recommendation of wage reductions, the protests of the miners and the mine-owners' lockout on 30 April of that year. This major war within the industry encouraged the more rapid development of production in Germany, Belgium, Holland and Poland. Furthermore, Germany and Poland gained substantial foot-holds in export markets. Reparations coal from Germany had also been hitting at British markets, and even after deliveries on this basis had ended, German exporters were able to go on exploiting the connections thus made, developing them into ordinary commercial relations.

But this was only a part of the story. The shift in the patterns of market supplies was greatly influenced by marked improvement in the technical efficiency of other European coal producers, while that of the British pits showed very little movement, as revealed in Table 4.

Table 4   *Output per man-shift (cwts)*

	Great Britain	Ruhr	Polish Upper Silesia	Pas de Calais	Belgium	Holland
1913	21·5	18·6	23·6	14·9	10·4	16·2
1924	17·6	16·9	14·3	11·4	9·1	14·6
1925	18·0	18·6	20·1	11·8	9·3	16·5
1926	18·5	21·9	23·7	12·9	10·1	19·5
1927	20·6	22·3	25·1	12·7	10·1	20·0
1928	21·3	23·4	26·9	13·4	10·9	22·9
1929	21·7	25·0	26·4	14·2	11·3	24·5
1930	21·6	26·6	26·5	14·2	11·3	24·5
1931	21·6	29·3	29·4	14·4	11·6	25·7
1932	22·0	32·1	31·2	15·4	12·0	28·4
1933	22·5	33·0	35·7	16·3	13·1	30·7
1934	22·9	33·0	38·5	16·6	14·4	33·2
Per cent increase 1913–1934	7	77	63	11	39	87

Source: *The British Coal Industry* (PEP)

What were the causes of this transformation of the relationships in productivity. Britain, the pioneer in this industry as in some others, seemed to be paying heavily for having been first. Specifically, two main features were pinpointed by PEP. The first was the far faster progress in mechanisation by our competitors who had entered the field later, and the second was their greater concentration of production in the larger and more efficient mines. A few years later the Reid Report (see below) was to return to these themes, drawing quasi-revolutionary conclusions.

But, first, to document the basis for the comments on mechanisation, Table 5 indicates the rate of progress by the main European producers.

Table 5   *Output and percentage of coal won by mechanical means**

	Great Britain		Ruhr		Polish Upper Silesia		Pas de Calais		Belgium	
	Million Tons	*Per Cent*	*Million Tons*	*Per Cent*	*Million Tons*	*Per Cent*	*Million Tons*	*Per Cent*	*Million Tons*	*Per Cent*
1913	24·8	8·2	2·5	2	—	—	—	—	—	10
1926	28·2	22·0	73·6	66	5·8	22	13	53	18·0	71
1927	59·4	23·0	95·0	80	7·2	26	16	65	22·3	81
1928	62·4	26·0	98·9	86	8·4	28	17·9	68	23·7	86
1929	73·1	28·0	112·8	91	10·6	31	21·1	72	24·0	89
1930	77·0	31·0	100·5	94	9·0	32	—	—	25·1	91
1931	78·1	35·0	82·1	96	—	—	—	—	25·0	93
1932	81·6	38·0	70·4	96	—	—	—	—	20·3	95
1933	89·2	42·0	74·7	96	—	—	—	—	24·4	96
1934	105·4	47·0	87·6	97	—	—	—	—	—	—

*In making a comparison of the progress of mechanisation in Great Britain and abroad it should be remembered that continental mines have been mechanised mainly with ripping picks and British mines with mechanical coal-cutters.

Source: *The British Coal Industry* (PEP)

Starting from a position well below that of Britain, the Ruhr industry increased its proportion of output of coal won by machines until almost all of it was gained by the use of pneumatic picks; Belgium made similar advances, but in Britain investment for this purpose was slower. Yet, PEP saw the concentration of production as being of even greater significance and named it as the 'chief explanation of the advance of productive efficiency in foreign coalfields'. In the mid-1930s there were still more than 2,000 mines in Great Britain; they raised an annual output of 220 million tons, or an average of about 100,000 tons each (though the potential capacity was reckoned to be almost double the actual output). Against this we can compare the Dutch mines of that time with annual figures of some 2 million tons each, the Germans averaging just under a million, and the Poles with about half of this level – though this included some 50 per cent of their pits producing a million tons or more every year.

PEP also carefully examined the proposition that the competition of foreign, and particularly Polish, coalfields had been subsidised in the past by the use of sweated labour. It found that the excuse was a myth. Sweated labour had once been a factor, but continental wages at the time were in fact generally on a par with British – higher in the Ruhr and the Netherlands, lower in France, Belgium and Poland, much the same in the Saar. But the incidence of labour costs per ton was in places 'much less' on the Continent than in Britain, owing to the higher productivity flowing from the more intensive mechanisation and the concentration of output, the effect being most marked in Germany and Poland. In 1933 the wage cost per ton in Britain was 8·12 shillings; for the Ruhr it was 6·35 and for Polish Upper Silesia 3·48. The troubles at that time were attributed to the false prosperity of the immediate post-First World War period engendering a false sense of security and in turn a lack of investment resulting in a leeway of productive efficiency. Before that war British coal had enjoyed a favourable margin in export markets of about 2 shillings a ton, owing to the higher output productivity of British mines over those of most other countries.

Until 1929, world consumption of coal continued to grow and so did world export demand in spite of the steady improvements in the economical use of fuel indicated (only for Britain) in Table 3 above. During the industrial depression there was inevitably a setback in the demand for export coal, and British producers suffered most since they had the largest interests in the export markets and were less able to withstand the more severely competitive conditions than the more efficiently organised continental producers. Adding to the difficulties were a growth of protectionism in many countries, and extra aid to exporters in Germany and Poland by such devices as special rail freight arrangements for export coal and subsidies of export prices by higher internal prices.

PEP concluded sternly that the amount of leeway to be made up was substantial, demanding improvements in technique and in pit concentration accompanied by the radical reorganisation of the structure of the industry to permit the concentration of output in fewer mines. And though it perhaps sought to mollify the owners by attributing many of the troubles of the industry to the false prosperity of the post-war period, adding coyly 'the coalowners, being only human, are not entirely to blame', the PEP authors nevertheless felt driven to an uncompromising conclusion. Without the combined benefit of both improvements in technique and radical reorganisation, no large or lasting proportion of the lost export markets could be recaptured by the expedients of trade agreements or other forms of political interference.

And events indeed were moving on, within a few years and after the ferocious flood of bloodletting in Europe, towards a reorganisation probably more thoroughgoing than the anonymous authors of the PEP Report had contemplated.

SUGGESTED FURTHER READING

Nef, J. U., *The Rise of the British Coal Industry* (Routledge, 1932)

Bernal, J. D., *Science in History* (Watts & Co., 1954)

Hobsbawm, E. J., *Industry and Empire* (Penguin Books, 1969)

Children's Employment Commission, Reports and Evidence, 1842 (Facsimile Reprint, Irish University Press, 1968)

Gregg, Pauline, *A Social and Economic History of Britain 1760–1965* (Harrap, 5th edn, 1965)

Report on the British Coal Industry (Political and Economic Planning, 1936)

CHAPTER 3

Towards nationalisation

... we have undertaken this task in our capacity as mining engineers, and [that] all our conclusions and recommendations have been formulated from our professional viewpoint
Paragraph 2 of *Coal Mining,* known as the Reid Report

Coal nationalisation was for many decades a political football in Britain, though now no one suggests returning the industry to private owners. In the last chapter I gave some indication of the appalling conditions that had developed in the pits by the middle of the nineteenth century. Reactions against these conditions, which remained dangerous and uncomfortable long after the law had been called on to improve them, included both strikes and calls for political changes. R. Page Arnot quotes the first annual report of the Scottish Miners National Federation, set up in 1886, as demanding co-operative production under state management. Drafted by Keir Hardie, the concluding paragraph ran :

> Ours is no old-fashioned sixpence-a-day agitation. We aim at the complete emancipation of the worker from the thraldom of wagedom. Cooperative production, under State management, should be our goal; as never till this has been obtained can we hope for better times for working people.

This was unanimously adopted by the delegates. The Miners Federation of Great Britain, formed in 1888, soon incorporated nationalisation of the coal industry as an integral part of its general policy, seen as the way to raise the standard of life of its members. Also unanimous was the adoption by the TUC in 1892 of this resolution :

This Congress, recognising the fact that well nigh three-quarters of a million workers are engaged in winning from the bowels of the earth produce that is national property, is of opinion that the enterprise should also be, like the Post Office, a State department and accordingly instructs the Parliamentary Committee to prepare a Bill embodying the foregoing facts and opinions.

The following year a resolution before the TU Congress very much in the tradition castigated by Keir Hardie, calling for a special tax for a fund for the relief of aged and infirm workers, was transformed by a forthright amendment into a reaffirmation of the demand for nationalisation. Again passed unanimously, the amendment said simply 'we re-affirm the position taken up by the last Congress and support the Parliamentary Committee in their efforts to have minerals nationalised'.

Some twenty years later, following a period marked by repeated bitter conflicts, a rank-and-file group in the Rhondda issued a pamphlet carrying forward the same features of policy. Its main aim was to unify the miners in South Wales to improve wages and conditions, but it included a programme of engaging in political action; its policy statement culminated in the objective 'to build up an organisation that will ultimately take over the mining industry and carry it on in the interest of the workers'. Entitled *The Miners' Next Step* and issued in 1912 by the Unofficial Reform Committee, it argued that if the workers were 'thoroughly organised in the first place, to fight, to gain control of, and then to administer that industry . . . this would mean real democracy in real life, working for real manhood and womanhood'.

Coal was in fact brought under wartime government control – though certainly not in forms that had been envisaged by the miners – in South Wales in 1916 to try to stave off incipient disputes, then in 1917 in the whole of the United Kingdom. This control was given up in 1921 after a further tempestuous period which included a threatened miners' strike, the setting up of a commission under the chairmanship of Mr Justice Sankey, a propaganda campaign by the TUC demanding that the mines be retained in the hands of the nation, a promise by the government to carry out the recommendations of the Sankey Report 'in the letter and in the spirit', and a final statement by that same government a few months later (18 August 1919) accepting the principle of the interim report but adding in the words of Lloyd George 'we cannot accept Mr Justice Sankey's final interpretation. His scheme for carrying that out we cannot accept'. The principle referred to had been a condemnation of the existing system of ownership and the proposal that some other system must be substituted, either nationalisation or a method of unification by national purchase and/or joint control. This was paraphrased by Lloyd George into 'a recommendation in favour of the unification and reorganisation of the industry'. What was the later interpretation by the learned judge that the Welsh wizard found so indigestible?

The Commission reported in stages. In the second stage, dated June, 1919, the recommendations made by Sankey included:

> I   . . . acquiring the Coal Royalties for the State and paying fair and just compensation to the owners.
>
> II . . . on the evidence before me that the principle of State ownership of the coal mines be accepted.

He added an itemised list of reasons, such as these:

> VIII   Coal is our principal national asset, and as it is a wasting asset it is in the interests of the State that it should be won and used to the best advantage.
>
> IX   The seams of coal are now vested in the hands of nearly 4,000 owners, most of whom are reasonable, but some of whom are a real hindrance to the development of the national asset.
>
> XV   Under State ownership there will be one owner instead of nearly 4,000 owners of the National asset, and the difficulties caused under the present system in regard to barriers, drainage, pumping, boundaries and support will largely disappear.

Yet, reflecting the state of the industry, this had been a deeply divided Commission. The first Report had recommended some reduction of hours, and increases in wages – in addition to the proposals on reorganisation; on each of these issues there were variations in the recommendations by some or other of the Commissioners. Similar divisions were repeated on the second stage. Seven members (including the Chairman himself) supported Sankey's Report and five made alternative proposals. In fact, not even the recommendations on reorganisation were carried out. After the government gave up its wartime control of the mines, the owners announced reductions in wages; attempts at resistance by the miners failed and the miners were defeated.

In the following period of continuing great difficulties for the industry – as briefly outlined in the preceding chapter – there were further official enquiries. In 1924 the Buckmaster Committee of Enquiry recommended an increase in wages and when the owners gave notice to end the resulting agreement the following year a further Committee of Enquiry was set up under Mr Macmillan, KC, with inconclusive results. As passions once more rose in the mining industry the government set up a Commission of Inquiry under Sir Herbert Samuel to suggest an early remedy for the serious economic state of the industry and recommend future organisation, and meanwhile made a temporary subsidy to the industry. When the Samuel Commission in 1926 recommended a reduction in wages and the ending of the subsidy, it precipitated a lockout of the miners, leading to a General Strike. For the miners, the dispute continued for nearly seven months, though eventually they had to yield, accepting a longer working day and reductions in wages.

Further work by the trade union movement itself on the theme of nationalising industries continued in the following decade with a memorandum prepared by the TUC and Labour Party, adopted by the TUC congress in 1933, leading up to plans for nationalising coal that were 'finalised' in 1936. As required by decisions at a number of national congresses, these plans included schemes for governing boards to include representatives of the workers in the industry – a contentious topic in labour and trade union circles, since many doubted if this type of arrangement was practicable. 'No industry' declared the memorandum, 'needs a fresh start so much as the coal industry', and it went on to advocate a British Coal Corporation working solely in the public interest. On the role of the trade unions themselves, it added :

The trade unions, however, must realise their own responsibilities if they are to play an adequate part in socialised industry. . . . A healthy discipline of workshop self-government must be developed in which authority is related to merit alone. It must be the discipline that is inseparable from effective teamwork.

Then in February 1937 a Nationalisation of Mines and Minerals Bill was introduced by the Labour MP Mr Batey, but on the second reading it was defeated in the Commons.

Nevertheless, during the Second World War – as in the First – the government found it necessary to take control of the industry, though in a form which was criticised since managers remained answerable to the owners as well as to the government. In June 1942, it published a White Paper on coal dealing with the demands of war production, the net wastage of labour from the pits, the return of men to the mines from the armed forces and the development of outcrops. Under the many pressures of the war it proposed to take full control of both the mining and the allocation of coal, setting up for this purpose a National Coal Board and establishing in each region a Controller with full responsibility for the conduct of mining operations in his region. Day-by-day management was left to the existing managers. Owners were to nominate a person to carry out the Controller's directions which would be mandatory. The workers were involved by the formation of pit production committees 'to assist pit managers to secure maximum output'. But the White Paper was also quite explicit in declaring that the wages and profit structure of the industry would not be fundamentally changed. The proposals came into operation the following month.

About the same time, the ownership of British coal resources in the ground became vested in the Coal Commission set up by the Coal Act of July 1938 and the private ownership of coal royalties came to an end. The function of the Commission was described as that of 'landlord' with a duty to promote the interests, efficiency and better organisation of the industry, but not to engage in mining operations other than searching and boring for coal.

THE REID REPORT

Politically, no doubt, it was the return of the Labour government in 1945 which directly led to the actual nationalisation of coal. But the heavy ammunition was supplied by the Technical Advisory Committee chaired by the mining engineer Charles Reid. Appointed in September 1944 'to examine the present technique of coal production from coal face to wagon, and to advise what technical changes are necessary in order to bring the Industry to a state of full technical efficiency', the Committee gave the impression of being overawed by the devastating indictment of the industry and the revolutionary conclusions conjured up by their own earnest labours. For the quotation at the head of this chapter comes from the second paragraph of their Report (the first being simply a re-statement of their terms of reference). After analysing in great detail the general causes of the low productivity of British mines, making drastic and far-reaching recommendations for technical changes, they 'carefully considered' whether they had thereby fulfilled their duty. In a tailpiece set out in bold type, this group of current and former mining managers and directors of colliery companies came to the conclusion 'that it is not enough simply to recommend technical changes which we believe to be fully practicable, when it is evident to us, as mining engineers, that they cannot be satisfactorily carried through by the Industry organised as it is today'.

The study had ranged over systems of mining coal, methods of winning coal, special requirements for power-loading, the support of workings underground, underground transport, ventilation, lighting, power underground and shaft winding. Moving their attention up to the surface, they examined layout and equipment, maintenance of machinery and provision of workshops. Ranging more widely the Committee went on to recommendations on training and education, how to improve labour relations, how to search for and use sensibly the national coal resources, then to plan for production by looking at problems on a coalfield basis rather than mine by mine.

Earlier they had carried out a historical review of British mining with particular attention to technical developments, breaking up the period into the years before and after 1926, with the comment that the stoppage of that year marked the end of a phase in the history of the industry. Regretting that no adequate steps were taken by the Mines Department or the Mining Association to bring home to the industry the serious competitive position that then developed, owing to marked progress particularly in Germany and Poland, the Reid Committee went on to remedy that lack themselves. Special studies were included in their report on technical developments in German, Dutch, Polish and American mining. Detailed comparisons led them to the conclusion that natural conditions in Britain were comparable with those in the Ruhr and Holland, affording no explanation of the much lower British output per manshift (OMS). Reasons advanced were then tabled under categories of relative financial resources, development of an excessive number of mines in Britain, better layout of roads in continental mines, their use of better (locomotive) haulage, better training of recruits, standardisation of coal sizes and short-term policies by employers. As a result, British mining engineers were handicapped and lacked the technical independence allowed to their continental counterparts. And the lack of co-operation between mineworkers and employers was also castigated with a kick at the British mineworker for not accepting the machine as a necessity. 'With fuller co-operation,' they concluded the comparison, 'OMS would have been considerably higher'. Then they went on to the detailed technical proposals mentioned briefly above.

But it was evidently the sense of the inadequacy of these recommendations in relation to the global problem of the organisation of the industry as a whole that had driven them on to their concluding chapter of bold recommendations, boldly presented, under the heading of 'The Conditions of Success'. Reiterating that 'it is not possible to provide for the soundest and most efficient development and working of an area unless the conflicting interests of the individual colliery companies working the area are merged together into one compact and unified command of manageable size, with full responsibility, financially and otherwise, for the development of the area', they carried the argument further :

> Moreover, if a comprehensive scheme of reorganisation along the lines we have recommended is to be carried through, we consider that an Authority must be established which would have the duty of ensuring that the industry is merged into units of such sizes as would provide the maximum advantages of planned production, of stimulating the preparation and execution of the broad plans of reorganisation made by these units, and of conserving the coal resources of the country. . . . A great pioneering task thus awaits the employer and the mining engineer, which is nothing less than the rebuilding of the industry on the most modern lines.

What of the men? They too had to be transformed.

> On the workmen and their leaders, too, falls a grave responsibility. They must combine with the mining engineer in an entirely new spirit of co-operation for a united effort to raise the productivity of the Industry to the highest possible level, and be ready to accept the obligations, as well as to claim the rights . . . they must welcome the introduction of machinery and do their utmost to see that it is made to give the greatest possible yield. . . .

Not so much a report, one might say, more an apocalyptic vision. Could these bold, radical ideas be given substance?

While the officially-appointed Reid Committee was still at work, Mr Robert Foot, chairman of the Mining Association, published a report to the colliery owners with his own proposals for the industry's reorganisation. Partially bowing to the wind of the then-current mood, he laid down the basic principle that the industry must be organised for national service, but rejected nationalisation as a counsel of despair. To provide for the required degree of reconstruction, modernisation and mechanisation he proposed a central control board with the object of achieving efficiency of production, workers' well-being, wage stability, reasonable return on capital and continuing development. Twenty 'governing principles' were put forward, including such features as taking a national view of the industry's responsibilities, making district arrangements for providing power or buying stores, integrating pits into a smaller number of units, absorbing displaced men elsewhere; workers were to be ensured a wage and stability of employment, joint committees were to be set up, finance provided for research – but, subject to faithful adherence to the principles, there should be no interference with the autonomy of individual colliery undertakings.

Like other defenders of the *status quo,* Mr Foot evidently regarded his plan as non-political, while proposals for radical changes were otherwise. 'If politics could be set aside,' his report concluded, 'and the owners and men's leaders discuss matters as partners in a joint enterprise, it might easily make all the difference in the world.'

Predictably, the colliery owners supported the plan, and within a month proceeded with drafting a constitution for the Central Coal Board, while the National Union of Mineworkers (NUM) rejected it as enabling the colliery owners to protect vested interests at the expense of the miners and the general public. A heavy responsibility for the long-continued fall in output rested with the owners, added the NUM, who went on to call for radical reorganisation under national ownership with heavy new investment. A month later, in March 1945, the Reid Report was published.

THE INDUSTRY NATIONALISED

Whether by coincidence or design, yet a further study of the industry appeared about the same time, by a man due to become President of the Board of Trade and, some years later, Prime Minister – Harold Wilson. Started as an intended Fabian pamphlet, this developed into a full-length analysis and policy proposal for a national corporation to own and operate all units of a socialised industry. The author saw this as combining national ownership and operation in the national interest with freedom from civil service methods, Treasury control and parliamentary concern with day-to-day operations. Replacing a situation where private ownership had become synonymous with non-enterprise, he envisaged a true *public enterprise* (italics in the original) giving the fullest freedom to men chosen on the grounds of their ability – and on no other ground – to exercise that ability.

Meanwhile the war in Europe was drawing to a close, ending officially on 8 May 1945. Later that month the Coalition government which had led Britain through most of the war resigned after the Labour Party ministers decided to withdraw and Winston Churchill announced a new Cabinet consisting of Conservatives, Liberal Nationals and non-party members. Its Minister of Fuel and Power, Major Lloyd George, almost immediately made a statement of general policy on coal reorganisation, 'in view of the vital importance of coal to industry and the export trade,' in these terms :

> . . . the Government . . . considered that the working, treatment and disposal of coal should continue to be conducted by private enterprise, provided they were planned in accordance with national needs and conducted with the maximum of efficiency, and had decided that a central authority appointed by the Minister of Fuel and Power and subject to his general direction, should be set up to insist upon the necessary measures to bring about the proper development and efficient conduct of operations in each

coalfield in accordance with the best modern practice . . . necessary . . . grouping . . . of collieries would be carried through, voluntarily if possible but otherwise by compulsion . . . policy . . . would provide the necessary sanctions for ensuring that the essential recommendations of the Reid report were carried through.

Again the Mining Association endorsed the attempt to maintain private ownership, accepting the policy and appointing a technical survey committee of mining engineers.

All these rearguard actions were swept aside by the landslide Labour victory in July 1945 – the majority was 146 – with a programme which included a clear commitment to public ownership of the fuel and power industries. On 1 January 1947 the coal-mines became the property of the nation. At each colliery was displayed a notice reading 'This colliery is now managed by the National Coal Board on behalf of the people'. This was the crucial legal step. But how far were the visions of the pioneers reflected in the realities that then developed?

SUGGESTED FURTHER READING

H. Townshend-Rose, *The British Coal Industry* (George Allen & Unwin, 1951)

White Paper, *Coal* (HMSO, June 1942)

Coal Mining. Report of the Technical Advisory Committee (HMSO, March 1945, Cmd 6610). This is often referred to as the Reid Report.

Coal Industry Nationalisation Act 1946

R. Page Arnot, *A History of the Scottish Miners* (George Allen & Unwin, 1955)

TUC Annual Reports 1892, 1893

Reports of the Sankey Commission (HMSO, 1919)

Report of the Samuel Commission (HMSO, 1926)

Robert Foot, *A Plan for Coal* (Mining Association of Great Britain, January 1945), with *Supplement to a Plan for Coal* (Mining Association of Great Britain, March/April 1945)

Election Manifesto (The Labour Party, 1945)

Harold Wilson, *New Deal for Coal* (Contact, London, 1945)

CHAPTER 4

What the nation took over

If we command our wealth, we shall be rich and free;
if our wealth commands us, we are poor indeed
Edmund Burke

Obviously, nationalisation meant taking over all the coal-mines, manufactured fuel plants and coke-oven and by-product plants owned by colliery companies. But there were many complications because the 800 companies were often operated in close association with other activities, notably the manufacture of iron and steel. The final tally comprised more than 1,400 collieries, 30 manufactured fuel plants, 55 coke-oven and by-products plants, 85 brick and pipeworks, 225,000 acres of farmland, and 140,000 miners' houses. Some of the more surprising assets acquired were shops, offices, hotels, swimming baths, wharves, coal sale depots, milk rounds, a holiday camp and a cycle track – but many of the non-mining assets were sold. In addition, 480 of the pits were 'small mines' employing fewer than 30 men underground. Generally these were granted licences by the National Coal Board (NCB) to continue in private operation.

As I mentioned earlier, the Coal Act of 1938 had already nationalised the coal deposits in the ground, which were administered by the Coal Commission as a landlord granting leases to promote 'the interests, efficiency and better organising of the coal-mining industry'. These assets passed to the NCB on vesting day. Those of the colliery companies were handled in a different way.

The companies themselves were not nationalised but most of their assets were transferred, except iron and steel works. Essential productive assets associated with working coal – mines, machinery, surface installations, offices and workshops, colliery coke-ovens and the like – were transferred automatically on vesting date. This brought all the large collieries and all the underground coal under one single ownership for the first time. Then there were two classes of optional transfers. One of these classes, including waterworks, wharves, housing, farms owned by colliery companies, were transferable at the option of either the Board or the owners, whether the other party agreed or not. The final class, comprising brickworks and any remaining assets of the companies or their subsidiaries, could be transferred at the option of the Board or the owner but only if the other acquiesced. Companies owning assets which could be affected were required to send in documents known as 'statements of interests'. So complex did all this group of procedures prove to be, and so diverse the structures of the companies, that even by the end of 1949, the Board did not clearly know the full extent of its assets.

Broadly, the Board set out to exercise options quickly for assets covered by the global sum to be fixed as compensation for the industry as a whole by a tribunal and for any assets needed for operating efficiently those that would be transferred automatically under the Act. What was the condition of the human and material resources involved in this great transfer?

The collieries themselves were often old, their reserves, in many cases, nearing exhaustion. In fact, over the following twenty years nearly 250 of them were closed down for this reason alone, and a further 80 for exhaustion of what were defined as 'realistic reserves'. The decline in technical standards (exposed in the Reid Report) had been followed by further deterioration of the industry during the war, so that its equipment was badly worn. Average output per pit was about 190,000 tons a year.

Sadly, the first annual report of the nationalised industry recorded that manpower at 690,000 was the smallest for fifty years. Furthermore, its composition was very worrying.

Of this total, 50,000 men were over 60 years of age, 300,000 were over 40 and 15,000 were 'Bevin boys' conscripted during the war and due for release within two years. Absenteeism at the coalface was nearly 20 per cent and output per manshift (all workers) was about 1·03 tons, compared with an average of 1·16 tons in the year before the war.

All this, at a time when coal was urgently needed!

Moving the Second Reading of the Nationalisation Bill in the Commons on 29 January 1946, Emanuel Shinwell, Minister of Fuel and Power, warned the House:

> . . . the existing position contains the elements of industrial disaster. In this context I speak without a trace of partisanship. The drift from the industry is appalling. The natural wastage cannot be overtaken by orthodox treatment. Relations between owners and men, generally speaking, are soured and embittered, and the efficiency of the industry relative to that of our Continental and other competitors is distinctly backward.

He went on to detail such features as the decaying state of the Lanarkshire coalfield in Scotland demanding development in other Scottish areas in order to maintain output; in Cumberland all the landward coals were exhausted, requiring new pits of great depth; in Lancashire the most accessible coal had been extracted, again demanding a great reconstruction programme and very deep new sinkings; many of the workings of the anthracite region in South Wales were uneconomic so that new sinkings were inevitable to meet internal and export needs. All these demanded a radical reconstruction of the mining industry 'both on its technical and its human side' on a unified basis, with heavy capital expenditure.

TECHNICAL FEATURES

Productivity was poor, as I have outlined in earlier chapters, and in some aspects comparisons with other countries were startling. For example, just before the war one haulage worker was needed for every 50 tons of coal produced in the USA (though with very favourable natural conditions), for every 20–25 tons in Holland, but for every 5 tons in Britain. There were still 21,000 pit ponies in use. Excessive numbers of men were engaged in handling materials, and the systems for taking men to and from the working faces were infrequent and far inferior in speed and suitability to those in competing overseas industries; the latter therefore gained advantage in saving effective working time and in expenditure of effort by the men. Generally, relatively little money had been spent on capital equipment, though the Reid Committee excused this on the grounds that the industry was in a perpetual state of financial embarrassment, earning low profits, feeling itself in a state of political uncertainty about ownership, unable to command adequate financial resources and receiving lower taxation allowances than the corresponding industries in other countries. Commercially the industry was hampered by an excessive multiplication of qualities and sizes of coal which in turn affected efficiency of operations, since there was no standardisation of sizes.

The principal system of mining in use was that known as Longwall Advancing. In this, as the name indicates, a panel of coal is extracted by working the coal-face on a broad front, leaving behind roadways servicing it. These roadways are supported by packs of stone and maintained for haulage and ventilation. But some pits used a system variously known as Room and Pillar, Bord and Pillar, Stoop and Room or Pillar and Stall. This is based on driving a number of narrow tunnels ('headings') into the seam parallel to each other, connected by cross-headings. Within this grid are left the pillars which are then extracted to the extent permitted by the need to support the surface. Yet a further system also in use in Britain was the Longwall Retreating, considered to be a kind of combination of the two just described. In this, headings are driven in the coal, but relatively wide apart, virtually forming large pillars. It is these that are then extracted, working backwards towards the roadway which had been used as the starting-point for the headings. The Reid Committee severely criticised the extensive use of the Longwall Advancing system on several grounds, such as difficulty in supporting the roof over the working area; the need for a rigid cycle of operations giving only one productive shift per day and being very vulnerable to absenteeism; lack of any indication of the quality of the field in advance of the productive face; leaving roadways in 'moving ground' and demanding quick salvage of materials and plant when the face reached its boundary. For highest productivity the Committee chose intensive Room and Pillar first, and a modified Longwall Retreating next.

The standard of lighting underground was also severely criticised by the Reid Committee as being too low, reacting adversely on production, safety and health. Flame lamps were still extensively in use, though they were obsolete, giving a very poor light – but of course they also acted as gas detectors – and general lighting of the face was recommended, supplemented as necessary by electric cap lighting. The percentage of coal mechanically cut underground did rise during the war, (though 20 per cent of the coal was still 'land-got'), and so did the proportion transported by conveyors. But, broadly, mechanisation at this stage was described by Mr R. F. Lansdown, the Chief Mechanisation Engineer (in a retrospective review ten years later), as 'a system of limited application concentrated in particular areas' and run with unsatisfactory standards of maintenance.

Only in a few parts of the country, notably South Wales, were techniques being applied for suppressing dust while cutting the coal. Supports in use at the face 'were rigid props set in conjunction with bars or with lids only' and a few yielding props were being tested out. The significance of these technical features will be more apparent in later chapters in which the progress of mechanisation is described with some backward glances for comparison. But death and injury rates can be immediately appreciated. Per 100,000 manshifts the death rate from all causes, underground and surface, was 0·30 in 1946, the higher component being from accidents underground with falls of ground as the major source. The rate had halved since 1913, but the 186·1 million tons raised in 1946 had still claimed 543 lives, while a further 2,335 men were 'reportably injured'; this term was defined as including persons suffering any fractures of the head or of any limb, or any dislocation of a limb, or any serious personal injury, or who were injured by any explosion, by electricity or by over-winding.

Some of the larger colliery companies retained the services of doctors, but this was largely to attend accidents and to advise the companies on claims for compensation for accident and disease. Only a few companies had a medical officer full-time whose job was to care for the general health of the men and ensure sound pit hygiene. In the whole of the industry there were only 22 state registered nurses. There were 37 rescue stations controlled by 31 separate bodies. A Mines Medical Service had been set up by the Ministry of Fuel and Power in 1943 but it was on a comparatively small scale. Then, towards the end of 1945, the minister directed the Miners Welfare Commission to provide a suitable medical centre at all new pithead baths. Some 20,000 men suffering from pneumoconiosis, mainly in the South Wales coalfield, had been suspended from work in the mines under a scheme introduced during the war. The number of cases certified outside South Wales was rising – from 445 in 1944 to 775 in 1946.

Coal preparation plants – for separating dirt from coal and usually grading it by size – were old and in the opinion of the engineers should have been replaced much earlier. Few companies had engineers responsible for checking the quality of output and maintaining the efficiency of the plant. Similarly, many of the coking plants were classified as obsolete and uneconomic, largely on the grounds that they were too small and had no facilities for blending coal to give the best results.

More generally, the scale of scientific research was small in relation to the magnitude and importance of the industry. There was a Fuel Research Station funded by the government, and attached to it were ten Coal Survey laboratories located in the coalfields. Methods of examining coal had been developed and standardised and coals could be tested at the research station in full-scale carbonising plant. There was also a small research programme at the British Colliery Owners Research Association. Yet overall, the 1947 NCB Report commented, 'the scientific inheritance of the Board was meagre'. What is more, the results obtained outside the government's research station, in the privately-funded laboratories, were closely guarded by their respective sponsors. Professor I. C. F. Statham, Professor of Mining at Sheffield, in a retrospective commentary ten years later, particularly picked out progress in spreading technical information, as a major change 'with attendant benefits to all concerned. Prior to nationalisation there was a natural diffidence on the part of many mineowners and mining engineers to disseminate information regarding the results of improved technique. . . . A similar attitude of secrecy . . . in regard to coal reserves . . . and geological features'. And apart from research, there was no comprehensive scientific service. A few of the colliery companies, generally the larger ones, had small laboratories, but many had none so that collieries could not deal with the minimum requirements of statutory regulations for safety nor test for quality of coal.

MINERS' CONDITIONS

It is often said that miners live in tightly knit communities and that their conditions of life are not very well known by the rest of their countrymen. Yet a wide-ranging series of surveys of the coalfields undertaken during the war resulting in reports published between 1944 and 1946 provided a wealth of information for those with eyes to read. The Scottish survey, for example, was carried out by a committee appointed in July 1942 with the following terms of reference, typical of those for other areas.

> To consider the present position and future prospects of coalfields in Scotland and to report —
> (a) what measures should be taken to enable the fullest use to be made of existing and potential resources in these coalfields, and
> (b) in this connection, what provision of houses and other

services will be required for the welfare of the mining community.

With maps, diagrams and tables the resultant reports – for all the coalfields – then went through the geological detail demanded by their first remit, but, meeting the second one, they also included most valuable information on the housing position, the housing requirements for the men needed to fulfil the plans for developing potential resources, the other services that would be needed and the further consequences in surface subsidence and in disposing of colliery refuse.

What did they find? Not all the housing fitted the stereotype of dismal dwellings that many have in mind when thinking of miners' cottages. The Committee quoted examples of miners' rows at East Wemyss in Fife and Newtongrange in Midlothian which were 'well-built and satisfactory . . . some people prefer them to the standardised new housing'. But the older examples certainly lived down to all the worst concepts that one could imagine. At Auchinleck in Ayrshire, Glencraig and Lumphinnans in Fife and elsewhere the report comments :

For drabness of appearance and atmosphere there is no grouping of dwelling houses we know which can compare with collections of the older miners' rows – dreary long lines of single-storey houses and between them only narrow strips of drying greens (though there is now no grass left, even if there ever was any), often with communal washhouses, conveniences . . . scattered over the 'greens'. Sometimes the atmosphere is polluted with the noxious fumes from a burning bing nearby . . . [often] condition is deplorable and the houses are worse than damp . . . usually only two apartments . . . little room for families, and much overcrowding. . . . Many of the older miners' rows are unfit for human habitation according to modern standards . . . many more which are of such a poor condition both in regard to the amenities available and their ability to withstand the elements that human beings should not be required to live in them.

Table 6   Illustrative extract from 'Regional Survey of the Coalfields, 1944 North-Eastern Coalfield' HMSO

Present Housing position of mining community in Sanitary Districts:

District 1	Extent of housing shortage among miners 2	Structural and other conditions of existing miners' houses 3	Amount of overcrowding in existing miners' houses 4	Brief summary of total housing requirements of the district 5
Urban Districts				
DODWORTH (M)	See column 4.	Colliery Co. Houses, 197 —Good. Council Houses, 150— Good. Private, etc., 250—Unsatisfactory.	Estimated 5 per cent of total houses (1,024 houses).	160 houses to replace unfit houses. 60 houses to replace overcrowding. Information not available for the needs of service men (newly married).
ROYSTON	Acute.	The majority of the houses are cottage type, small gardens (if any), lack of bathrooms, etc. The condition of them is fair.	Approx. 52.	390 applications for houses.
DEARNE (M)	Very acute. It is estimated that approx. 1,000 houses are needed at the present time to make good housing arrears.	Generally speaking the existing houses are fairly modern, a great proportion having baths and all having w.c. accommodation. There are no back to back houses in the district.	Estimated that 100 cases of serious overcrowding exist at the present time.	The Council plans to build 1,000 houses in the two years immediately after the war ends.

Rural Districts

DONCASTER	Acute housing position at present complicated by presence of 2,150 official evacuees and 750 Bevin boys in private billets, also unknown numbers of unofficial evacuees. Estimated shortage in mining areas not less than 500 houses.	On the whole very good. Mainly minor defects except for six to seven hundred houses at Askern without baths and 80 wooden bungalows at Edlington in which the main fabric has outlived its usefulness.	See column 2 as to presence of Bevin boys and evacuees. During the 1936 Overcrowding Survey, 270 houses were found legally overcrowded. Position worse than in 1936.	See column 2.
KIVETON PARK	At least 300 houses are required.	3,000 of the 4,700 houses in the district are of pre-1914 standards with no bath, hot water system and with outdoor w.c.'s. A very large proportion of the houses require minor repairs. This applies to modern Council and Colliery houses as well.	There are no reliable figures available at the present time. The Overcrowding Survey figures are out of date.	At least 600 houses are required to abate overcrowding, to replace unfit houses, to provide accommodation for workers travelling from other districts, to provide accommodation for newly married couples, etc.
WAKEFIELD	Estimated shortage of houses —350.	Insufficient light and ventilation, unsuitable and insufficient amenities. Excessive dampness, general dilapidation due to war conditions.	Houses overcrowded 117 (occupiers approx. 550).	(a) 700 to replace houses scheduled for demolition. (b) 300 to meet requirements first three years. (c) 50 to abate overcrowding.

Table 6—continued

ROTHERHAM	At least 1,000 houses.	A large number of houses in need of repair. This applies to Council houses, Colliery-owned houses and privately-owned houses.	Varies from day to day. Aggravated in last few months by influx of evacuees. Many colliery houses with two or more families. Several gross cases of overcrowding have occurred.	Not less than 2,000 houses required. This includes replacement of unfit houses, relief of overcrowding and other needs.
TADCASTER	Parishes of Swillington and Preston—141. Parish of Micklefield—38.	These do not appear to be any different from other houses. In the parish of Preston there are houses which will have to be dealt with under Section 11 of the Housing Act, 1936.	No recent figures relating to this.	No figures available for whole of the Rural District, but there is a programme for 50 houses in the Tadcaster Town and 50 houses in the parish of Swillington, for the first year, and a programme of 167 houses for the second year which embraces the parishes of Askham, Bryan, Barkston, Copmanthorpe, Church Fenton, Micklefield (48), Saxton and Ulleskelf.

Similar features, differing in detail, were found elsewhere in many mining areas. Table 6 is an extract from the survey of the North-Eastern coalfield, by way of example. Naturally, it was not mining districts alone that were suffering from bad housing; and the table makes it clear that the worst features were not confined to houses owned by collieries. In fact, some of these were listed among the better ones. Yet the general depressing pattern was clear. And a large number of these 'drab', 'uninhabitable' homes were among the assets which the new administration was to take over on behalf of the nation.

The colliery companies proved to have a wide variety of salary and wage systems. When they were checked over by the new officers, it was found that different companies paid miners, surface workers and administrators at wildly different levels for identical jobs. Some employees had emoluments in kind, such as a free house, free coal, or even a free gardener. A few favoured sons had salaries and perks that were extraordinary for their time. Among the people that the first board declared redundant, under varying conditions according to the nature of the contract, were some with salaries of £8,000, and one with tax-free perquisites worth a further £2,550. At that time – for comparison – the Prime Minister's salary was £10,000 a year and the Chairman of the incoming National Coal Board was paid a salary of £8,500. The average manual worker's wage in mining and quarrying was £5 15s. 8d. per week in April 1947. Some companies had superannuation schemes for staff, others had none.

In some cases coal distributors had been favoured by coal-owners with contracts giving them the sole exclusive rights to dispose of the whole output of a colliery or the output for one area. Exclusive agencies of this type controlled the sales of over 30 million tons of coal (and of quantities of manufactured fuel) per year in 1946. These contracts hindered the free market sale of the coal, or could have hampered planned marketing programmes by a national authority.

There were pithead baths provided by the Miners Welfare Commission for about half the miners in the country. This was a statutory body operating under the aegis of the Ministry of Fuel and Power. Drawing a penny on every saleable ton from the colliery owners and a shilling from the owners of coal royalties (who were at the time of nationalisation the Coal Commission) for every £1 of royalty, it provided a range of welfare services. In addition to the pithead baths there were canteens (in all they covered 97 per cent of the workers in the industry), recreation schemes, community centres, educational and cultural activities, rehabilitation centres, convalescent homes and hospital schemes. Some welfare services were also provided by some colliery companies. As far as they went, these were among the positive features taken over. At the Vesting Day ceremony, Mr Shinwell also referred to the human resources, picking out notably 'the most competent army of mining technicians in the world' – possibly a strange tribute in view of the repeated analyses of technical backwardness of the British industry. Yet the Reid Committee had, if not actively praised, at least muted its criticism of mining engineers, excusing them with the comment that 'the atmosphere of financial stringency, and the lack of broad vision, which, it must be admitted, generally surrounded the direction of the British coal industry, provided the mining engineer with little encouragement to formulate bold schemes'. Nevertheless it did indeed criticise them for insularity of outlook.

Finally, in respect of training of new entrants to mining, the Reid Committee wrote of 'some provision' for training in safety methods; but training was mostly based on learning directly on the job, particularly on haulage operations. It was severely criticised as far inferior to that of the Continental industries. Furthermore, standards of qualification of all grades of mine officials were condemned as 'far too low' and their experience as 'too narrow'.

Analysing, in 1949, the problems and achievements of the minister and his first board, an American commentator, Assistant Professor R. Vance Presthus (of the University of Southern California), saw the job, in essence, as 'the technical rehabilitation of the most vital element in the British industrial complex'; its most relentless opponent as '*history*, in the form of the legacy of fear and suspicion arising from the embittered labor relations of the past and the technological obsolescence of the industry'; and the value of what was taken over as 'a bankrupt enterprise'.

These, then, were the resources which were to be welded together and developed on behalf of the nation into a thriving, unified industry serving the national interest, the consumers and its own workers.

SUGGESTED FURTHER READING

Regional Surveys of the Coalfields (HMSO). A series of publications issued between 1944 and 1946

Debates in Parliament on the Coal Industry Nationalisation Bill in 1946, notably the speech by the Minister, Mr Emanuel Shinwell, moving the Second Reading in the Commons, 29 January 1946

Coal Industry Nationalisation Act, 1946 (9 & 10 Geo 6. Ch. 59)

National Coal Board, *Annual Report and Statement of Account for the year ended 31 December 1946* (HMSO, 1948)

National Coal Board, *Annual Report and Statement of Account for the year ended 31 December 1947* (HMSO, 1948)

'National Coal Mines', *The Colliery Guardian,* 3 January 1947, p. 13, (in an account of Vesting Day ceremonies and speeches)

Presthus, R. Vance, 'British Public Administration. The National Coal Board', *Public Administration Review,* Vol IX, No. 3 (Summer 1949)

National Coal Board. The First Ten Years. A *Colliery Guardian* publication (Undated, but presumably 1957)

CHAPTER 5

The first Board

The Dawn of a New Era
> Motto on banner of Risca Lodge, South Wales
> Area, National Union of Mineworkers

The Coal Industry Nationalisation Act, 1946 – defined as 'an Act to establish public ownership and control of the coal-mining industry and certain allied activities – declared simply in its first paragraph:
'there shall be a National Coal Board . . . .' The Board was charged with the duties of

1 working and getting coal in Great Britain;
2 securing the efficient development of the coal-mining industry;
3 making supplies of coal available, of such qualities and sizes, in such quantities and at such prices as might seem to it best calculated to further the public interest in all respects.

It was required to carry on such activities as it thought fit to discharge these duties. Named activities were searching for coal, treating and selling it, producing any necessary goods and utilities, training employees, education and research. A general clause mopping up anything omitted from the specific list added 'any activities which can advantageously be carried on by the Board with a view to making the best use of any of the assets vested in them by this Act'.

Naturally, the Board was given power to enter into transactions, but was also to secure the safety, health and welfare

Fig. 3 The banner of the Risca Lodge, South Wales Area, National Union of Mineworkers. (John Gorman Collection.)

of employees and to gain the benefit of the practical knowledge and experience of its workers. It was the Board's 'duty' to consult with the organisations of employees to conclude agreements for 'establishment . . . of joint machinery' for settling terms and conditions of employment, and to consult on health, safety and welfare, and operations. It had to organise its affairs so that the revenues should meet the outgoings (including payments to the Exchequer as directed by the minister for redeeming debt and paying interest, and establishing a reserve fund), 'on an average of good and bad years'.

The minister would appoint the Chairman, Deputy Chairman and seven other members. Broadly, the Board had power to govern its own affairs but the minister had authority, after consulting with the Board, to issue general directions in relation to matters appearing to him to affect the national interest. A further limitation was that the Board had to come to the minister for approval on the specific issues of programmes of reorganisation or development involving substantial outlay on capital account and also on training, education and research. Consumer councils were set up for both industrial and domestic consumers – both with suitably general terms of reference and entitled to notify the minister of their conclusions after any relevant investigation. On a primary vesting date (not named in the Act) the assets directly concerned with coal winning were to be transferred to the Board without option. As mentioned earlier, there were also two further categories of assets. Of these, one could be transferred at the option of the Board or the owners, and the other at the option of the Board or the owners subject to arbitration if there were an objection on either side. Compensation was basically to be satisfied by issuing government stock. For capital outlays, including working capital, the minister could advance, on his own authority, £150 million within five years or, during any later period, 'such amount as Parliament may hereafter determine'. Among the miscellaneous provisions was a duty to establish machinery for settling terms and conditions of employment and consulting on other allied matters such as safety, health and welfare. The aim was, as Mr Shinwell put it during the Commons debates, to set up a 'model employer with the full glare of limelight upon its activities'.

Although the Bill received the usual parliamentary treatment, with amendments in the Commons Standing Committee, then at the Committee stage in the Lords, Mr Shinwell, introducing the Lords amendments back to the Commons (10 July 1946) and conceding that there had been compromises, felt able to conclude : 'I can find nothing objectionable in the form of the amendments'. The first Act received the Royal Assent on 12 July 1946, but many of its provisions were altered or extended by a series of further Acts that proved to be necessary.

The names of the Board's members were announced in March, obviously to get things moving as quickly as possible, but the formal appointments were made by a new minister, Hugh Gaitskell, on 15 July 1946. As soon as the names were announced, the Board immediately started meeting as an Organising Committee and toured the coalfields to discuss plans with leading men in the industry, including sounding out some of them for key posts in the future organisation. The members were :

Lord Hyndley, Chairman
Sir Arthur Street, Deputy Chairman
Lord Citrine, in charge of Manpower and Welfare
Mr Ebby Edwards, in charge of Labour Relations
Sir Charles Ellis, in charge of Scientific Department
Mr J. C. Gridley, in charge of Marketing
Mr L. H. H. Lowe, in charge of Finance
Sir Charles Reid and Mr T. E. B. Young, jointly in charge
of Production

What sort of people had been appointed to govern this first major essay in public administration of a socialist-minded government? Understandably, the Board was constructed to be a balance comprising men committed to the success of the basic concepts, mining experts, experienced administrators, and also – as a matter of practical politics – men drawn from the board-rooms of the colliery companies. The Chairman had been Managing Director of the Powell Duffryn Group for fifteen years (and also for most of that time a director of the Bank of England). Sir Arthur Street was a distinguished senior civil servant, formerly Permanent Under-Secretary for Air, Secretary of the Air Council throughout the war, then Permanent Secretary of the Control Office for Germany and Austria until he took up his appointment with the Board. Labour interests were strongly represented by Lord Citrine, who had risen through many trade union posts to be General Secretary of the TUC for twenty years, and Ebby Edwards, secretary of the miners union (actually the Miners Federation of Great Britain until 1 January 1945, when it became the major component of the National Union of Mineworkers).

In May 1947 Lord Citrine was appointed Chairman of the Central Electricity Authority and resigned from the Board. He was replaced two months later by the secretary-general of the National Union of Distributive and Allied Workers, Sir Joseph Hallsworth, who had also seen service on many national and international committees on labour problems.

Placed in charge of applying science to the industry was a distinguished scientist, Sir Charles Ellis, FRS, Professor of Physics at King's College, London, with experience of science administration in parallel service as adviser to the Army. Finance was to be controlled by L. H. H. Lowe, partner in a firm of chartered accountants, who had held government posts as Director of Finance, having this position in the Ministry of Fuel and Power for a large part of the war. Marketing was placed in the hands of another director of Powell Duffryn (and other companies), J. C. Gridley. Direct mining engineering expertise was to be provided by T. E. B. Young, with experience in several coalfields and former Production Director at the ministry, and Sir Charles Reid, father of the famous report, and also a former Production Director at the ministry where he had moved from the position of General Manager and Director of the Fife Coal Co. Ltd.

In addition to the above departments under the direct supervision of Board members, the Board set up two further departments. To look after general administrative services was the job of the Secretary's Department, and legal work was made the responsibility of a Legal Department.

Choice of a date for taking over the industry was delayed a few months. But in October the minister 'consulted the Board about fixing the vesting date' urging on it the view that the takeover should not be postponed beyond 1 January 1947. This was certainly rushing the infant NCB, since its organisation in the coalfields was incomplete, and on the vesting date over 800 companies would cease to be responsible for the conduct of the industry. As the Board realised, it would have colliery managers in charge of pits but without any clear authority to which they could look for instructions.

Since the industry had very little office accommodation in London, the Board did not even have a suitable headquarters office to inherit (unlike the transport, electricity and gas industries). An early vesting date meant an enormous administrative load, but delay would carry 'psychological dangers' of continuing uncertainty and in some cases divided loyalty. On balance the Board agreed to the date urged on it and the minister formally announced it in the Commons in November, leaving the Board six weeks in which to complete its arrangements.

Guided by the recommendations of the Reid Report, it intended to group pits into planning units to be known as areas which would become the main units of management. Forty-eight of these units were created and Table 7, reproduced from the first Annual Report, shows how the original collieries were grouped. To avoid over-centralisation, a further intermediate set of authorities was created known as divisions. Based largely on the seven natural geographical groups formed by the coalfields, with an additional dividing line broadly along the Yorkshire/Nottinghamshire county boundary, the eight divisions set up also carried forward the grouping previously used for the regional organisation of the Ministry of Fuel and Power. They were due to have divisional boards similar in composition to the national one with minor changes, and to be collectively responsible to the national Board.

Since, at the vesting date, these new authorities had not been fully set up, while those which were in being could not all hope to assume detailed control immediately, the Board

Table 7   *Original NCB Colliery Groupings (Divisions and Areas)*
From NCB Annual Report for the year ended 31 December 1946

Division and Area	No. of Collieries	Approximate Annual Output (Million Tons)	Geographical Area
1 Scottish Division	187	21·9	
Area No. 1	42	6·3	Fife and Clackmannan
Area No. 2	19	3·1	Lothians
Area No. 3	51	4·7	Stirling and Lanark
Area No. 4	33	3·5	Lothians
Area No. 5	42	4·3	Ayr and Dumfries
2 Northern Division	213	34·0	
Area No. 1	12	3·2	N.E. Durham
Area No. 2	16	4·6	Mid-East Durham
Area No. 3	9	3·2	S.E. Durham
Area No. 4	22	3·6	S.W. Durham
Area No. 5	30	3·3	Mid-West Durham
Area No. 6	45	5·0	N.W. Durham
Area No. 7	29	2·8	S. Northumberland
Area No. 8	25	4·2	Mid-Northumberland
Area No. 9	13	3·1	N. Northumberland
Area No. 10	12	1·0	Cumberland
3 North Eastern Division	117	37·4	
Area No. 1	13	5·4	Worksop, Notts.
Area No. 2	12	7·3	Doncaster, Yorks.
Area No. 3	13	5·6	Rotherham, Yorks.
Area No. 4	13	4·8	Carlton, Notts.
Area No. 5	13	3·1	S. Barnsley, Yorks.
Area No. 6	18	3·3	N. Barnsley, Yorks.
Area No. 7	18	2·7	Wakefield, Yorks.
Area No. 8	17	5·2	Castleford, Yorks.
4 North Western Division	75	12·6	
Area No. 1	24	5·1	Manchester, Lancs.
Area No. 2	17	2·5	Wigan, Lancs.
Area No. 3	10	2·2	St Helens, Lancs.
Area No. 4	16	0·8	Burnley, Lancs.
Area No. 5	8	2·0	North Wales
5 East Midlands Division	102	32·6	
Area No. 1	15	4·7	N. Derby and Notts.
Area No. 2	10	4·9	N. Derby and Notts.

Table 7—*continued*

5	*East Midlands Division*—cont.			
	Area No. 3	9	5·5	N. Derby and Notts.
	Area No. 4	17	4·1	N. Derby and Notts.
	Area No. 5	21	4·6	N. Derby and Notts.
	Area No. 6	10	3·0	N. Derby and Notts.
	Area No. 7	11	2·6	S. Derby
	Area No. 8	9	3·2	Leicestershire
6	*West Midlands Division*	60	16·1	
	Area No. 1	20	5·7	N. Stafford
	Area No. 2	17	4·3	Staffordshire— Cannock Chase
	Area No. 3	9	1·4	S. Stafford and Shropshire
	Area No. 4	14	4·7	Warwickshire
7	*South Western Division*	222	21·8	
	Area No. 1	66	3·7	Swansea (Anthracite Area)
	Area No. 2	24	2·5	Maesteg — South
	Area No. 3	32	3·7	Rhondda — Wales
	Area No. 4	23	2·6	Aberdare
	Area No. 5	18	3·1	Rhymney
	Area No. 6	40	4·8	Monmouthshire
	Area No. 7	6	0·8	Gloucestershire and Forest of Dean
	Area No. 8	13	0·6	Somerset and Bristol
8	*South Eastern Division*	4	1·3	East Kent—No separate Area organisation

Note.—'Small Mines', which the Board were not to manage themselves, are excluded throughout.

made special transitional arrangements with the colliery owners, acknowledging that this was achieved 'through the good offices of the Mining Association'. Divisions appointed the managing director or some other senior official of each company as a 'Controller' responsible to divisional or area management, but carrying on the work of the colliery or other unit until the new organisation was operating effectively and authority could be transferred. Though nationalisation is much discussed in political terms, the areas were of course large commercial organisations, albeit accountable to the higher authorities, with annual turnover of around £10 million each. By the vesting date the divisional boards had been appointed and were ready to take on their responsibilities, but in general had not organised the area managements, so that they had to operate the transitional system.

Almost immediately the industry had to meet a major crisis due to an exceptionally severe winter. The railways had difficulty in moving coal, so that government emergency measures had to be introduced. Exports were prohibited; over a large part of the country industry, except for essential services, was stopped from using electrical power; troops and army lorries were brought in to assist in moving fuel; bull-dozers had to be used to clear railway lines and roads. The Board reported that in the East Midlands division during this period 820 army lorries were in use for transporting coal and at one time there were no fewer than 12,800 railway wagons loaded with coal that could not be moved. Simply getting the mineworkers to and from the collieries was in itself a major operation; in some places, it was reported, where buses could not run because of snow and ice, men walked several miles to work. Emerging from this trial by freeze-up, the industry found that, thanks to the efforts made to meet the crisis, total output of coal during the months of February and March was over a million tons more than for the corresponding months of the previous year.

There had been a drop in production during the war, but the trend had been reversed in the autumn of 1946. Among the first objectives of the new Board was to focus the attention of colliery managers and divisional production directors on short term reorganisation in order to increase output within months. Aiding its efforts was the greatly improved relation-ship with the miners ('the mineworkers were in good heart' said the second annual report – a one-sided comment but evidently capturing the mood), but technical and operating changes needed to be made too. Managers were instructed to introduce modern machinery to the face wherever early results were reasonably assured and to be ready to apply new recruits. Pressure on the government led to agreement that miners would not be called up for military services (general conscription of men into the Armed Forces did not end until 1960), training centres would be expanded, priority would be given to the coal industry for machinery and other supplies, an extra share of aluminium houses would be allocated to mining areas, and local authorities would be asked to give priority to miners.

GREAT DEMANDS . . . . AND THE RESPONSE

The first NCB acknowledged that it had made great demands on the men and women of the industry in that first year of national ownership. They were 'demands not only for hard work but for a conscious change in long-standing habits and attitudes of mind'. How had it set about it and what were the results? In 1947, deep-mined output, at 187 million tons, was 6 million tons up on the previous year. Added to the coal produced from opencast sites, it made up a total of 197 million tons, only 3 million tons short of the government target set early in the year. Manpower increased – despite the raising of the school-leaving age in that year – attendance improved and so did output per manshift (Table 8).

Table 8 *Manpower and Output 1938–47*

Year	Saleable Output Deep-mined Coal (Million Tons)	Average Number of Workers (Thousands)	Absenteeism (Per cent)	Output per Man-shift (All Workers) (Tons)
1938	227·0	781·7	6·44	1·14
1939	231·3	766·3	6·94	1·14
1940	224·3	749·2	8·27	1·10
1941	206·3	697·6	9·03	1·07
1942	203·6	709·3	10·39	1·05
1943	194·5	707·8	12·43*	1·03
1944	184·1	710·2	13·62	1·00
1945	174·7	708·9	16·31	1·00
1946	181·2	696·7	15·95*	1·03
1947	187·0	711·4	12·43	1·07

*Owing to changes in the definition of 'wage earners' in 1943 and again in 1946, the later figures are not strictly comparable with the earlier. However, the effect of the changes is less than 0·5 per cent.

Consequently the Board was able to build up consumers' stocks during the year and resume exporting on a small scale. And this was achieved despite the reduction of working days due to introducing the five-day week – one of the fruits of work by the Joint National Negotiating Committee. (A later NCB/NUM agreement in October 1947 extended working hours in response to a government appeal to all basic industries for increased output. It was agreed that the extra hours might be worked by arranging an extra half-hour a day or by Saturday shifts.) The Joint National Negotiating Committee formed part of the arrangements set up under the National Conciliation Scheme adopted by agreement with the NUM in December 1946, largely continuing those already agreed some three years earlier.

Although one of the Board's first objectives was to change the spirit of the industry, dispelling old bitterness, removing old grievances, it also had to apply some pressures to improve productivity, reduce over-manning on haulage and – as part of the five-day week agreement – increase daily tasks in various ways on a basis agreed between management and NUM delegates at Pit Production Committees. On this front not all was sweetness and light. Despite the improvements noted above, the Board found the response to the appeal for extra tasks 'disappointing'; it actually led to unofficial strikes in some coalfield districts, the most important being the dispute at Grimethorpe colliery in Yorkshire causing a loss of output of over half a million tons and even drawing in the National Board, the Minister of Fuel and Power and the national NUM before it was settled in a rather inconclusive way and the men returned to work.

During the year the Board raised the minimum weekly wage and increased the pay of the lower-paid workers. It also relieved mineworkers of the need to pay for pithead baths – this former payment must indeed have been felt as an intolerable imposition in view of the nature of the work – and thus at last brought British practice into line with that elsewhere. These various changes resulted in the cost of producing a ton of coal rising by 4s. 3d. and the estimated cost overall amounted to an annual rate of 62½ million pounds. Actual colliery losses were over £9 million. The report for 1947 gives the results overall summarised in Table 9. Commenting on these figures, the Board pointed out that the deficit was not a charge on the taxpayer and that it planned to 'overtake' it

Table 9

	£	£
Colliery Losses	− 9,203,905	
Ancillary Profits	+ 3,016,605	
Operating Loss		− 6,187,300
Other Transactions		
Loss on Imported Coal		− 1,697,992
Provision for compensation for loss of office		− 406,192
Other Income		+ 156,177
Interest and Interim Income payable		− 15,120,279
Net Deficit		− 23,255,586

in later years. The Board was, of course, obliged under the terms of the Act to make the £15 million payment and had to incur the loss on imports which would not have fallen on private coal-owners. The latter would not have been burdened in the same way with the interest payments and could have covered part of the deficit by not distributing any dividends. True new investment for additions and improvements took some £16 million.

In a carefully balanced statement fully in tune with the purposes behind nationalisation, the Board discussed its plans for the future, pointing out that it could make coal much cheaper simply by closing down unprofitable pits or selling a little less of some coals at much higher prices. But it saw itself as guided by the need to act in the national interest, to have regard to social costs, and to accept a responsibility to posterity by not immediately working all the accessible seams and leaving the more difficult ones for the future. These aims had to be combined with normal business considerations based on the strictly economic effects of any action on the industry. Both led to the conclusion that the industry had to be made as efficient as possible, producing the quantities and kinds of coal that were needed as cheaply as possible, with a fair reward for management and men.

BUILDING AN ORGANISATION

In this first working year, the NCB had to maintain (or improve) production, take over staffs and assets of 800 separate organisations and set up the beginnings of permanent organisation in areas, then covering whole coalfields in the divisions, and finally nationally, including the establishment of small staffs of specialists at headquarters. Out of 800 units motivated by normal profit-making incentives it had to create a public service with a new pattern of loyalty and sense of public responsibility.

Rightly, the Board discussed the problems and perspectives in the 1947 Report, examining what this demanded of the miners in the way of self-discipline, of managers in the need to respond to the changed psychological environment, and of itself in respect of its duties as a good employer. Administratively, it stated its aim to be to evolve an organisation as flexible and efficient as the work demanded. It was based on the principle of responsibility for policy at the centre and devolution of managerial responsibility to the parts, optimistically defined in the phrase 'to delegate but not to diffuse responsibility'. Problems ranged from such workaday issues as finding accommodation and opening bank accounts, to such major ones as determining policy to employees, deciding which unions to recognise and building up conciliation and consultation schemes. The Board negotiated the establishment of the five-day week, but also a scheme for extended working hours in response to an appeal from the government for this effort to meet the country's economic difficulties. The scheme for longer hours was explicitly to be operated in such a way that it did not interfere with the full carrying out of the agreement on the five-day week. The extra hours were worked in some parts of the country as an extra half-hour per day, in others as Saturday work. Other measures to increase output were the extension of drift mining (which is economical and gives high yields per man) and recruitment of volunteer workers from Europe, who were trained in English language and culture as well as the more direct needs of their intended jobs.

A new scientific organisation was built up since, in its own words, 'the scientific inheritance of the Board was meagre'. In the first place, it concentrated on giving day-to-day service on scientific control operating at the collieries. Main concerns were safety and quality control. Regulations on safety demanded extensive sampling of the dust in mines for tests for non-combustible matter, testing of the atmosphere for the percentage of methane and testing of miners' lamps for their light output. In addition mobile gas analysis units were provided in some divisions to help colliery staff in dealing with emergencies such as explosions or underground fires. As a basis for preparing a new price structure linking price with coal quality, a rapid chemical survey was carried out during that first year. Progress was made in servicing, with scientific testing, the many collieries which had no such service before nationalisation, and arrangements were made for checks on the quality of exported coals. Routine analytical control at the so-called 'washeries', where coal is in varying degree separated from incombustible matter, had been very patchy. The NCB began to extend the testing of raw coal, products and discards and set itself the objective of covering in this way all its washeries to ensure consistency in the quality of the marketed coals and to get the maximum yield of saleable coal from the plants. For the first time, in many areas, coal seams were systematically investigated by screening their coals into different sizes, dividing these into classes of specific gravity and determining the ash and sulphur content in each case as a basis for establishing the specification of new plants and the coal to be produced from them.

The Coal Survey organisation, which had been attached to the Department of Scientific and Industrial Research – where it was in effect a free service to the old coal-owners – was transferred to the NCB as a national unit with laboratories on the coalfields but controlled centrally from headquarters and now charged against the industry. Apart from this, there was only a small research staff taken over from the former British Colliery Owners Research Association and one large company, and other projects in progress in universities, hospitals and four co-operative research associations.

Another new organisation was the National Miners Welfare Joint Council which incorporated the former Miners Welfare Commission, added two representatives of the NCB, and thus integrated all welfare activities. A structure of committees was set up in divisions and areas with representatives of the unions throughout at all levels. Immediate plans were adopted for starting to build pithead baths at 120 collieries; the aim was to provide baths at all new collieries and at all existing collieries with a reasonable span of life in order to provide for the half of the total mining labour force who did not have them at that time. The NCB also encouraged divisional boards to stimulate interest in both mining and wider education in a variety of ways, including foreign exchanges and visits. Wisely, it saw the work of consultative committees as part of this process and urged that it should be brought home to the man at the coal face. Further contributions were made by launching a magazine, *Coal,* a monthly newsreel and an exhibition in London opened by the Prime Minister and partly staffed by working miners. These measures were supplemented by Board members visiting the coalfields, staff conferences and a summer school and a wide range of cultural activities such as art exhibitions, dramatic societies, displays of handicraft and paintings that went on tour to leading municipal art galleries throughout the country.

The Minister of Fuel and Power remained responsible for making regulations concerned with safety, with specialist mines inspectors as his agents. But the Board appointed a Standing Committee of Board Members to stimulate safety activities and a national network of safety officers with a Chief Safety Officer at headquarters. Research was continued on the control of strata undermined by colliery workings, a first installation of fluorescent lighting was completed at Chislet Colliery (as the Reid Committee had recommended for general reduction of accidents, improving health and comfort of workers – and production), and a range of trials was initiated to suppress dust which otherwise increases risks of explosion and of pneumoconiosis. Headed by a Chief Medical Officer, a comprehensive health service was set up throughout the country with medical officers also at divisions. The Board adopted as policy the appointment of doctors to large collieries and to groups of collieries, supported by state registered nurses and working in medical centres at all new pithead baths, while existing pithead baths would be adapted to provide medical centres. It set up a committee under the Scientific Member to deal with industrial diseases and to support a government-appointed committee specifically dealing with pneumoconiosis. In respect of rescue stations, ambulance services and first-aid arrangements (training and competitions) the Board took over services of varying levels of thoroughness and training and started plans to improve and extend them.

Yet even while building these foundations, the industry suffered the traumatic experience of four major colliery accidents during that year; the most serious was that at the William Pit, Whitehaven, Cumberland. Overall, sadly, both the number of deaths and the number of those 'reportably injured' were higher during this first critical year than in the previous two years.

Improvement of the quality of coal was seen as an urgent necessity. At that time coal was in short supply and customers could not be too critical. But, looking forward, the Board saw that it would be increasingly difficult to sell the poorer grades of coal as the supply situation altered. It therefore began a drive to produce cleaner coal (including the scientific survey mentioned above), setting up a coal preparation organisation, ordering new plant, sending engineers to improve the operation of existing plant, emphasising also to all workers – particularly the coalface workers – the importance of cleaner coal, and in some cases simply re-starting plants discovered to be standing idle. By the end of the year, forty-five plants were ordered or projected and 140 new schemes were under consideration to clean about 60 million tons of coal annually. Two major consumers reported clear-cut technical benefits from these efforts – the Great Western Railway in performance per engine-mile and the Central Electricity Board. For marketing, seventeen former district selling schemes were replaced by a new marketing organisation, where the headquarters staff formulated policy as advisers to the Board, while selling was handled in divisions and areas according to the special characters of the individual coalfields. During this period, too, the Board had responsibilities for controlling coal supplies in accordance with government instructions. Then, though coal continued to be mainly sold through the same channels as before nationalisation, the Board reduced the number of distributors and ended the exclusive selling agencies for collieries (referred to in Chapter 4).

All these were essential steps to meet immediate needs. But the Board had to prepare plans for the future development of the industry. These preparations were seen as falling naturally into three main subjects:

1　reconstructing old pits and sinking new ones;
2　forecasting the demand for coal;
3　settling a long-term policy for prices and wages.

The first wave of fifty-two major schemes with a total value of over £22 million, approved during the year, included old schemes of former colliery companies re-examined and new schemes. They were of various types – new collieries, reconstructions, the replacing of four smaller collieries with a composite single one, and some surface works, distributed up and down the country. In the forecasting exercise, the Board sought to examine trends such as the big increases by power stations and gas works, the move towards smokeless fuel, the need to produce coal for export of exactly the kinds that importing countries wanted, and the way that demand for British coal would be influenced by its price, abroad and at home.

On coal classification by size and quality – which would have to be the basis of a rational price structure – the Board simply adopted in principle the results of earlier work by both the British Colliery Owners Research Association (for size groupings) and of the DSIR (for quality). But the overhaul of this price structure and of the wage structure, as well as the long-term planning of output coalfield by coalfield, were simply set out as objectives; in both these areas the NCB could only begin to tackle the problems since they proved to be complex and inter-related.

'Ancillary activities' – carbonisation and briquetting, brickworks, estates, small mines – though on a smaller scale, still demanded attention. With the pits, the Board had taken over coke ovens producing about two-fifths of the national output of hard coke; the iron and steel industry had about equal production and about one-fifth remained in the hands of private companies. Demand for coke from both iron and steel and from the domestic market was heavy and increasing. A thorough survey showed that many of the plants would have to be replaced or extensively repaired. They included one battery of ovens built in 1882, though these were found to be in better condition than some less old but less well maintained. A Carbonisation and Briquetting Branch was set up, linked to production and marketing members of the Board. Simply to maintain output was estimated to need 175 new coke ovens to be built each year, while expansion would obviously call for more and modernised equipment. Gas was being supplied to the gas industries in many areas but developed plans for carbonisation involved extending these in a co-ordinated way as well as extending the marketing of the by-products – tar, benzole, sulphate of ammonia – which were a large fraction of the national output of those products, at that time widely used in the chemical, pharmaceutical, plastics, paint and dye, and fertiliser industries. About $1\frac{1}{2}$ million tons of briquettes and ovoids were made in 1947 in thirty plants, many of which used coal otherwise unsaleable. Here, no firm plans were announced except for a general intention to develop the output as rapidly as possible.

The Board became the owner and manager of property on a large scale, using estate managers who were generally appointed from staff transferred from the companies, and retaining the property for much the same reasons as the original owners bought them – to carry on colliery operations, for welfare, recreation and housing, and sometimes to be able conveniently to deal with subsidence damage.

Some of the press were not slow to recognise the magnitude of the 'great pioneering task' and the extent of the achievement. The daily with the largest circulation, the *Daily Express,* rhetorically asked in its editorial comment :

> What has Britain to show for the first year of the great experiment which was to prove the concrete worth of socialism? Dearer coal for the consumer, smouldering discontent among the producers; recruitment for the mines at a standstill; opportunities for politicians to grind their axes at the expense of the nation; burdens on the taxpaying citizen who cannot see where his liability will end.

The *Daily Telegraph,* though showing some elements of understanding, nevertheless headed its comment 'A Dark Report'. Its judgement was :

> On the whole it is a pretty gloomy prelude to the adventure of our greatest industry. It shadows the future with 'ifs'.

Probably the oddest combination of comments came from the *Yorkshire Post,* which headed its news report 'State's costly year as mineowner' and commented :

> The NCB is failing because the spur of the profit motive is gone.

Less than a week later, its editorial on the first quarter's results for 1948, when the Board made an operational profit of over £4 million, leaving a surplus of half a million after paying interest and interim income charges, ran :

> Coal has made a profit in the first quarter of 1948. It would have been surprising had it been otherwise. The question is whether coal is being raised at the right price. Coal production is a monopoly and a fairly simple adjust-

ment in the price will at any time convert a loss into a profit.

This shows remarkable flexibility by leader-writers, though possibly demanding similar pliability on the part of readers. Broadly the *Financial Times,* the *Manchester Guardian* and *The Times* gave factual reports and comments which showed appreciation of what had to be done. The news report in *The Times,* for example, included an acknowledgement that :

> The increase of 4s. 3d. a ton represents no more than the general increase in costs in British industry in 1947 despite special expenditure which the Board had to incur. . . . If the Board had been free to close unprofitable collieries it would have been easy to improve the financial results. . . . Long term planning is an immense task. Nothing comparable to it will ever before have been attempted in the industry.

And the *Manchester Guardian*'s news report recognised :

> The Board had to do some uncommercial things last year. Apart from the five-day week it had to maintain whole coalfields in operation at a loss because of the need for coal. Before coal mining passed into State ownership it received a subsidy from the Exchequer of £27,500,000 but now the industry must stand on its own feet.

For the rest, opinion was generally divided along largely political lines – which in practice meant that the balance of press comment throughout the country was more often hostile than understanding. And a sour postscript to the launch of the industry under public ownership was provided in 1949 in academic terms by Assistant Professor Presthus who observed in the face of the clear evidence to the contrary that I have shown earlier in this chapter that 'the Board appears to have operated without much regard for the day of financial reckoning which confronts it . . . the Board does not seem to have been designed for success according to commercial standards'. In fact, over the following ten years it consistently made a profit on colliery operations, though these were sometimes wiped out by other charges.

Regrettably, in 1948, Sir Charles Reid whose devastating analysis of the privately-owned industry had contributed so strongly to the final stages of the movement towards nationalisation, resigned 'following a disagreement with the Board about certain arrangements which it is making to review its organisation'. Sir Geoffrey Vickers, VC, was appointed a Board Member in his place. Sir Charles stated that he had no confidence in the Board or the organisation it had set up, which he considered cumbersome and uninspiring; without radical alteration – he proposed complete decentralisation – nationalisation, in his view, would prove a disastrous failure. Though state ownership was essential to full technical reconstruction of the industry, the organisation itself must be founded on sound business principles. The Board immediately announced a committee to take stock of the position, consisting of two outsiders, Sir Mark Hodgson, president of the Confederation of Shipbuilding and Engineering Unions, and Sir Charles Renold, president of the British Institute of Management, with Sir Robert Burrows, a part-time Board Member, as chairman. It also issued a reply to the charges pointing out that Sir Charles Reid (jointly with Mr T. E. B. Young) had been primarily responsible for planning the technical reorganisation, and that the creation of a strong yet flexible organisation could only be achieved by patient and steady development. Furthermore, and surprisingly, it stated that the membership and terms of reference of the committee appointed to review the situation had been approved by Sir Charles.

Inevitably, the *Daily Express* found this a monumental condemnation of the government's inefficiency, the *Financial Times* 'a verdict against the whole system on which we are now dependent for coal'. Yet when the committee reported, it was not wholly uncritical, and though it made suggestions for improvement, it generally endorsed the decisions on organisation, notably the grouping of collieries into areas of 4 million tons output each and the grouping of coalfields under eight divisional boards. And a few years later the board again submitted itself to critical outside examination, with the results shown in the following chapter.

SUGGESTED FURTHER READING

Coal Industry Nationalisation Act 1946 (9 and 10 Geo 6. Ch. 59)

National Coal Board, *Annual Report and Statement of Account for the year ended 31 December 1946* (HMSO, 1948)

National Coal Board, *Annual Report and Statement of Account for the year ended 31 December 1947* (HMSO, 1948)

H. Townshend-Rose, *The British Coal Industry* (George Allen & Unwin, 1951)

Press comments on NCB *Annual Report,* 14 July 1948

Presthus, R. Vance, 'British Public Administration. The National Coal Board', *Public Administration Review,* Vol. IX, No. 3 (Summer 1949)

CHAPTER 6

Expanding horizons

When we build, let us think that we build for ever
John Ruskin, *The Seven Lamps of Architecture*

Subjected to a constant barrage of hostile criticism, the industry under its new form of control nevertheless made progress, though in a strangely erratic way, as the results of the Board's first eleven years (Table 10) indicate. Until the middle of the 1950s, coal remained virtually the only important source of energy in Britain. Demand rose so fast that the industry was unable fully to meet it and coal had to be imported from America. A marked change in trend was felt in 1957 in both exports and inland consumption. This is discussed in the next chapter. But what had happened during the decade of expansion?

First, let us make an important digression. Half-way through this important formative stage, there came to power a government consisting of men who had fought nationalisation of the coal industry or only reluctantly accepted it – the Conservative government of 1951. In the debate on the King's Speech, Labour opposition spokesman Hugh Gaitskell felt sufficiently concerned at the possibility of damage to the new form of the industry to appeal to the new political masters to accept nationalisation. Geoffrey Lloyd, the new Minister of Fuel and Power, readily gave the assurances requested. After recalling that the Conservatives had already acknowledged that coal nationalisation was 'here to stay', he continued:

I can repeat those words with responsibility. Once you have accepted a nationalised coal industry you cannot sit around

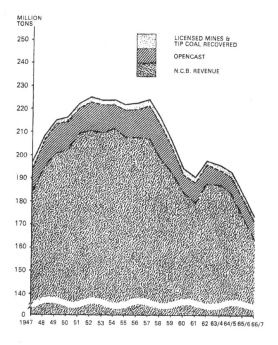

COAL OUTPUT (mill. tons) YEAR	REVENUE	OPENCAST	LICENSED MINES & TIPS	TOTAL
1947	184.4	10.2	2.2	196.8
48	194.6	11.8	2.1	208.5
49	200.7	12.4	1.9	215.1
50	202.3	12.2	1.7	216.2
51	209.4	11.0	1.8	222.2
52	210.7	12.1	2.1	224.9
53	209.8	11.7	2.0	223.5
54	211.4	10.2	2.2	223.8
55	207.8	11.4	2.4	221.6
56	207.3	12.1	2.7	222.1
57	207.4	13.6	2.7	223.7
58	198.8	14.4	2.7	215.9
59	192.5	10.8	2.8	206.1
60	183.8	7.6	2.3	193.7
61	179.6	8.5	2.3	190.4
62	187.6	8.1	1.7	197.4
63/4	187.0	6.1	2.1	195.2
64/5	183.2	7.0	2.3	192.5
65/6	173.5	7.1	2.2	182.8
66/7	163.8	7.1	2.1	173.0

Fig. 4   Coal output 1947–57. (NCB.)

looking at it with neutral or semi-hostile eyes, much less mess around with it. Once you accept it in the national interest you have to back it and do your level best.

The only reservation indicated by the new minister was that he would give no assurance as urged by Gaitskell – that there would be no change in the structure without full consultation

Table 10 *The Board's progress, 1947–57*

	1947	1948	1949	1950	1951	1952	1953*	1954	1955	1956	1957
Coal Output (million tons)											
Deep-mined	186·5	196·7	202·7	204·1	211·3	212·7	211·8	213·6	210·2	209·9	210·1
Opencast	10·2	11·7	12·4	12·2	11·0	12·1	11·7	10·1	11·4	12·1	13·6
Total	196·8	208·5	215·1	216·3	222·3	224·8	223·5	223·6	221·6	222·0	223·6
Average Manpower (thousands)											
Faceworkers	288	293	296	288	287	294	293	290	289	286	285
Other workers	423	431	423	409	411	422	420	417	415	417	425
All workers	711	724	720	697	699	716	713	707	704	703	710
Recruitment	93	74	52	55	73	75	52	61	61	66	71
Wastage ...	66	66	69	76	63	54	62	61	67	62	65
Net change	+27	+ 8	−16	−21	+ 9	+22	−11	—	− 6	+ 3	+ 6
Attendance (all workers)											
Shifts worked per man											
per week	4·69	4·71	4·67	4·72	4·81	4·79	4·67	4·71	4·68	4·65	4·61
per year	244	245	243	245	250	249	243	245	243	242	240

Table 10 *The Board's progress, 1947–57—continued*

Productivity

Tons per manshift												
Faceworkers	...	2·856	2·922	3·020	3·110	3·175	3·147	3·216	3·257	3·275	3·333	3·363
All workers	...	1·074	1·108	1·160	1·194	1·210	1·193	1·224	1·231	1·225	1·232	1·231
Tons per man year	...	262	272	282	293	302	297	297	302	299	298	296

Earnings (per manshift)†

		s. d.	s. d.	s. d.	s. d.	s. d.	s. d.	s. d.	s. d.	s. d.	s. d.	s. d.
Faceworkers	...	36 10	41 1	43 1	44 10	48 6	54 0	56 10	59 7	63 7	69 4	75 1
All workers	...	28 10	33 1	34 4	35 6	38 10	43 2	45 5	47 9	50 11	55 8	60 0

Colliery Financial Results (per ton of saleable coal)

		s. d.	s. d.	s. d.	s. d.	s. d.	s. d.	s. d.	s. d.	s. d.	s. d.	s. d.
Costs	...	41 3	45 7	45 0	45 5	49 2	56 9	59 2	61 11	67 3	74 5	81 6
Proceeds	...	40 3	47 3	47 11	47 10	51 2	57 3	61 2	63 6	68 0	77 0	82 0
PROFIT (+) OR LOSS (−)‡	...	−1 0	+1 8	+2 11	+2 5	+2 0	+0 6	+1 11	+1 7	+0 9	+2 7	+0 7

Consolidated Financial Results (£ million)

PROFIT (+) OR LOSS (−)	...	−23·3	+1·7	+9·5	+8·3	−1·8	−8·2	+0·4	−3·8	−19·6	+12·8	−5·3

*New definitions of manpower and attendance were introduced in 1954. The relevant figures for 1953 have been adjusted to the new basis.

†Including the value of allowances in kind.

‡Operating profit or loss, i.e. before paying interest.

and agreement between the Board and the NUM. The Board itself made no reference in its Reports to the change of political stewardship and, as far as one can assess, the undertaking given by Geoffrey Lloyd was honoured.

Returning to the record of this first decade, we see that production rose annually until 1952 in a drive for coal at any price, although the reconstruction programme was also making increasing demands on men, capital and management. Many of these reconstruction projects were of great size and complexity and were not completed until about 1960. The result was that output stagnated over the second half of the first decade of public ownership – deep-mined output remaining in the region of 210 million tons a year.

Meanwhile the Board had published in 1950 a *Plan for Coal,* aiming for a deep-mined output of 240 million tons a year in the period 1961-5. Six years later, it published a major revision entitled *Investing in Coal,* based on experience in the major colliery schemes intended – as economic adviser E. F. Schumacher put it – to 'breathe new life into an old industry', and scaled down the objective to 230 million tons by 1965 rising to 240 million by 1970. Two features had led to this revision. What Schumacher described as the main lesson was establishing that 4 million tons of capacity were lost every year in this extractive industry, needing to be made good by completing major schemes simply to maintain existing capacity. This is, of course, a basic difference from a normal factory. For in this case, a large part of the factory has to be uprooted and moved on every working day and the factory finds from time to time that its raw material has simply disappeared (at a geological fault, or a 'washout') or has become so thin, contorted or otherwise difficult to work that continuing with that part of the factory would be uneconomic; sometimes, indeed, for this reason, the factory has to shut down. The second finding was that there were simply not enough skilled people to cope. In more formal terms, 'the task of creating new capacity both for replacement and expansion, when added to the ever-present task of increasing current output, would strain to the utmost the industry's resources of organising and engineering talent'.

The first aspect of this 'lesson' – that capacity is continually being lost – was well known in principle; but while pits were privately owned it had never been possible to calculate a figure for the rate at which the process developed. The figure derived, corresponding to losing about 2 per cent per year of productive capacity, agreed well with that found by a contemporary international group, led by Sir Harold Hartley, examining Europe's growing energy needs. The investment requirements for creating one ton of coal production capacity a year also proved to be very similar – £12 10s. for the Continent, £10–£12 for Britain. Increasing capacity was seen as the main need, since the pits were considered to have enough men by 1953. Pits were divided into planning classifications comprising those from new sinkings or major reconstructions where output was rapidly increasing, those with lesser reconstruction or continuing without major change where production was more or less maintained, and a group expected to close down within the next fifteen years because their resources would be exhausted. The last of these categories was of course simply being run down; in them, output in 1951 was 95 per cent of that in 1947, and in 1955 further reduced to 88 per cent of the figure for 1951. In fact, by the end of 1956 about 140 of the original 980 collieries taken over had been closed down.

'One reason,' said the Reid Report, 'why continental countries have been able to forge ahead in productivity per man is the fact that they have been able to command adequate financial resources with which to carry out major technical improvements.' That lesson, too, was learnt. Schumacher quoted a twenty-fold expansion of investment in comprehensive reorganisation of existing mines or in new collieries or drifts within an early period of six years. Total investment over the period 1947–9 averaged £23 million a year, rose to an annual average of over £60 million in the next six years, and reached £100 million in 1955. Forward plans for the following decade involved capital expenditure of £1,000 million, broken down in this way :

1   Capital cost of current output for replacement and routine development needed 2*s*. 6*d*. a ton, integrating up to a total of £276 million;
2   'Ancillary activities' not directly connected with coal production would require £140 million;
3   'Colliery associated activities' – exploratory boring, central washeries but also welfare such as pithead baths, canteens, medical centres – had £34 million allotted, equivalent to 3*d*. per ton;
4   £550 million was available for major schemes, reckoned to produce about 50 million tons of new capacity. But 40 million tons of capacity would be lost over that period, so that the net gain was cut to the difference of 10 million tons.

What did the various objective indices show of progress over the first ten-year period? The increases in production over the first five years, followed by the stalemate in the second similar period due to effort being more heavily switched to new projects, have already been mentioned. For the same reasons productivity per manshift overall and for faceworkers followed much the same pattern. Nevertheless, output per manshift for faceworkers rose over 10 per cent and the earlier reconstruction schemes led to a rise in surface productivity of nearly 30 per cent. In an article in the *Colliery Guardian*'s review of the first ten years, Sir James Bowman, Chairman at that time, was able to quote a 'significant fact'; it was that 'productivity in British coal mining, which before the war used to be lower than that of its Continental competitors, is now higher; the best coalfields in Europe, such as the Saar, cannot compare with our best; and the worst, or least productive, are much inferior to our worst or least productive . . . this *general superiority* of the British coalfields has been established only since the war'. (The rise in productivity in fact became much more marked in the following years, although the West Germans pulled ahead of the UK in output per manshift.)

To its great credit, the Board, with the co-operation of management and men, almost halved the death rate and did almost as well in reducing the figure for serious reportable accidents. After the first year, it consistently made an operating profit on its colliery operations, though this was not always reflected in its overall financial results. For, unlike a private company financed largely by shareholdings, it had had to raise all its capital by borrowing from the government at fixed rates of interest, much of this being compensation capital for assets of very low productivity; and, also unlike a private company, it had to pay interest regularly without having the option of declaring no dividend on shares in bad years. After paying interest, it had six years when it made a profit and four of making a loss, so that the Board emerged from the period with a relatively small positive balance.

On the cost of coal, the Board was frequently criticised, though any balanced check on its performance for the proceeds per saleable ton of coal showed that from 1949 as a base, increases remained well below the official Board of Trade Index of Wholesale Prices (all items) with which they could be legitimately compared. Similarly the frequent wild accusations of continuing strikes in the industry were exaggerated, though they had better foundation than the comments on costs. Broadly, from 1933 to the end of the war the number of working days lost through stoppages in coal-mining alone was equal to that for the whole of the rest of British industry. After that the graphs diverged and coal began to account for only about half as many days as the rest of industry. Even in strike-prone 1955, when over a million working days were lost in mining and the Board ruefully commented that disputes had cost the industry more coal than in any year since nationalisation, the lost days in other industries rose sharply to almost three million. Despite all that had been done to produce new kinds of relationships in the industry, Bowman was justified in pointing to deeply ingrained strike habits of the past within mining, as well as the general 'strike climate' of the country as a whole in assessing the progress that had been made. In this context, Bowman even felt able to quote the greatly improved ratio of days lost in mining compared with those in the rest of British industry as his first example of the transformation that had been made in coal, where 'the "forces of decline" were gradually being overtaken by the new "forces of expansion" ', so that, in another metaphor, 'new life has been put into its old body'.

To the opponents of nationalisation, the process of taking an industry into public ownership meant (and often today is still taken to mean) the creation of excessive, overpaid bureaucracies. A popular newspaper cartoon of the period, for example, showed a large group of pin-stripe-suited men at a colliery watching a single miner walking to the pitshaft. The caption was an explanation by one of the stage army of bureaucrats to another, 'That's the man who digs the coal'. Cutting through the illusions of this deliberately fostered fantasy world was the report of a high-powered committee commissioned by the Board to review its organisation and chaired by the head of the largest British company (Imperial Chemical Industries Ltd), Alexander (later, Lord) Fleck, FRS. On one issue after another the Committee found the widely publicised criticisms to be exactly the opposite of the truth. Though the Fleck Committee did make its own criticisms and proposals for some areas of reorganisation, the introduction to its report included these comments:

> . . . difficulties unparalleled in any other industry of which we have knowledge . . . much of the criticism of the Board and their organisation has been ill-informed . . . it is remarkable how much has been done . . . new organisation brought into being in a matter of months. Those who performed this task did a remarkable job in the face of difficulties that could have been overwhelming. Any criticisms that we may make in the course of our Report must not be allowed to detract from these considerable achievements . . .
>
> We are satisfied that the main structure of the organisation – Headquarters, Divisions, Areas and Collieries – is sound. And so is the principle of 'Line and Staff' on which the organisation is based.

(This principle is that there must be a clear line of command and responsibility from the Board to the coalface; attached to each authority in the 'line' are the staff needed to get the work done, constituting with that authority a level of management.)

What of salary levels? In relation to both the responsibilities of the job and the qualities and standing they should have, Board Members' salaries were judged inadequate and 'substantial increases' recommended. Perhaps comments on over-generous salaries were more valid at other levels? Fleck and his colleagues found that technical people in the coalfields in several of the grades which should be represented at headquarters enjoyed perquisites from the old days – free house, free coal, services of a gardener and others – which they lost on coming to London. So they were actually worse off, and the Fleck Committee wanted the Board to remove these impediments to the transfer of good people from the coalfields to headquarters: which also implies its views on the level of staffing in London. Often it was too low. Production Department for example needed strengthening with more staff.

FURTHER RECOMMENDATIONS

Other areas where the advisory committee found the critics had stood facts on their heads so that it was necessary to invert the criticism to get the situation back securely on its feet, were on tightness of control over capital schemes and on the more general issue of centralised control. Capital expenditure, it found, needed tighter rather than looser control by headquarters; far from being held too long for examination, 'the schemes should have the thorough sifting and testing to which they would be subjected by a commercial concern in private industry', and therefore extra technical staff were needed.

Far from strictly imposing its bureaucratic diktats on the lower levels (as in the press fantasy), the Board was criticised for imposing too little. It was congratulated on the decision to decentralise but told that it must nevertheless enforce policy decisions. Where the Board had felt it wrong to force the adoption of budgetary control and standard costs on those reluctant to use them, Fleck reprimanded it for its mistaken attitude and added for good measure a potted lesson on decentralisation.

> . . . decentralisation means that each level of management specifies clearly the powers which may be exercised by the level below it. Having done so, it leaves the lower formation free to exercise those powers. But each level of management must see that the policies which it lays down are punctually and effectively carried out . . . not by interference in detailed or day-to-day matters, but by modern management techniques of approved programmes followed by periodical reports and reviews of progress and by physical inspections.

One other detail merits attention. Palatial offices were another of the myths being sedulously cultivated – based in this case on the fact that divisions had sometimes taken over disused, sometimes decaying, old stately homes in the country to accommodate staff. The Advisory Committee noted that several divisions in fact suffered from inadequate offices, adding a recommendation that a determined effort should be made to house them properly and economically.

On central issues of organisation, Fleck and his colleagues noted that the Board had first been set up with members each responsible for a department. Later this 'functional' character had altered and members ceased to be separately responsible for departments. The Committee now recommended that, apart from the Chairman and Deputy Chairman, a full-time Board member should both actively exercise a wide view on all the issues coming before the Board, and have a special field of responsibility or interest. He would not be head of a department but would have an executive head responsible for day-to-day management of a department, while the Board member established clear and comprehensive policy, reviewed it from time to time, ensured that the department was properly organised and generally watched over its progress. The Board should be expanded to the twelve permitted by statute, consisting of a Chairman and Deputy Chairman, six full-time members with defined fields of responsibility and four part-time members – to combat the tendency to self-centredness of the industry. The part-time members would have already proved themselves in some phases of industrial leadership, holding leading positions, and be representative of the best industrial thinking. Fleck himself added a personal recommendation, evidently not endorsed by his colleagues, that the Board should be increased to a total of eighteen, allowing for another Deputy Chairman, two more part-timers and three more full-time members, suggesting that this would give greater flexibility in operation.

The Committee as a whole urged the use of organisation and methods teams at several levels to help improve efficiency of office operations and added a discussion of a theme of some general importance in the running of public bodies. In private industry, it noted, one important yardstick of performance was financial results, though this could be a crude one if used only by itself. In the coal industry, however, a pit, area or division making a profit is not necessarily more efficient than one making a loss. Results depend not only on efficiency of management and production, but on such factors as thickness of seams, depth of workings, geological conditions, the inherent quality of the coal or the state of the market for that coal. Even if attention is switched to criteria such as output, output per manshift or costs of production, the conditions varied so much throughout the country that it was not reasonable to set a common standard. Consequently, the Committee urged, standards should be 'tailor-made' with a set of standards for each pit. Management should set them by reference to what the pit ought to be able to achieve; they should be realistic and attainable, agreed rather than imposed, and varied as changes in conditions occurred. The details, naturally, were related to conditions of the coal industry, but similar problems will arise in any public body which is subject to direction on grounds of public policy, so that ordinary profit-and-loss commercial criteria may not be wholly appropriate and the governing board will have to establish standards for assessing performance of management and men.

The report was published by the Board early in 1955.

Since it included recommendations for reorganising the Board itself, the recommendations were 'brought to the attention of' the Minister of Fuel and Power who agreed to the recommendations in this area. The new appointments were very quickly made, and the new Board, after examining the report, also accepted most of the Committee's recommendations in consultation with management and unions. The Chairman remained Sir Hubert Houldsworth, who had earlier been Chairman of the highly successful East Midlands division, with Mr J. Bowman (former Vice-President of the National Union of Mineworkers, then Chairman of the NCB Northern division 1950–5) as his Deputy Chairman. When Sir Hubert died in the following year, Bowman was appointed Chairman.

TECHNICAL DEVELOPMENTS

Apart from the major schemes, development continued in many aspects of mining techniques with the aim of improving both safety and productivity. For supporting the roof at the coal face, timber props were progressively replaced first by rigid steel props, then, as a better means of meeting the needs of mechanisation at the face, by introducing the so-called 'yielding' supports – mainly hydraulic but some based on friction. But in a contemporary article, Dr H. L. Willett, Deputy Director-General of Production, explained that despite the improvements in props and bars for supporting the roof, the most efficient use of manpower applying the then-modern coal-getting machines demanded self-advancing supports, generally with horizontal rams for pushing the prop forward; several of these systems were under trial. Developments in using explosives included firing shots in rounds of six at a time for increasing efficiency and safety, trying out new explosives with cooling salts as safety ingredients mixed into the explosives themselves, and firing shots with the explosive under water pressure assisting in suppressing dust and usable for softening coal so that it could be worked by plough. In a few pits, firedamp was being drained from the strata surrounding the seam being worked, to produce safer conditions, and applied as a fuel in various ways. Great progress was being made in suppressing dust during cutting coal and dirt by a range of methods of water infusion, wet cutting, and spraying, and by physico-chemical aids such as wetting-agent addition to the water or a mixture of wetting agent and 'soluble' oil, or water and foam.

Though in the first five years mining research formed part of a wider programme of one centre, this function was separated in 1952 when a Mining Research Establishment was set up. The Board then found that developing prototype and experimental machinery demanded yet a further centre to supplement the resources of manufacturers of mining machinery. By 1956 a Central Engineering Establishment (CEE) was virtually complete for designing and producing trial machines. At that date, the Board had 330 scientists and scientific technical officers, and 65 engineers engaged on research and development projects at the three central establishments. The functions of CEE were also to apply the results of research, improve existing equipment, prepare specifications, evolve standards, and further encourage and co-operate with British manufacturers in developing and introducing new machines and techniques.

Reviewing developments in 1957, the Chief Mechanisation Engineer, Mr R. F. Lansdown, differentiated between progress of the 'more orthodox' methods of coalface mechanisation – using coal-cutter and conveyors – where the Board had by that time brought up the tonnages cut to around 90 per cent of the total, and a great variety of machines capable of simultaneously getting and loading coal. Such machines included ploughs, cutter-loaders based on jibs and chains, and cutter-loaders based on rotary heads. The variety of working conditions was found to demand a corresponding range of machines. By the end of 1956, 920 of these power-loading machines were reported to be in use.

Introducing the much tougher armoured flexible conveyors, which could be moved forward without dismantling, solved many of the difficulties involved in using coalface machinery and led to the development of further types of loading machines. In the 1956 Annual Report of the Board, the Anderton Shearer received a particularly rapturous mention.

During that year, it had cut over 10 million tons at an average output per manshift at the face of 5·8 tons raised and weighed. It was based on a rotary drum cutter with a 'plough' attached to divert the cut coal on to an armoured conveyor. Some were big enough to cut out the whole seam in one operation. Then, in addition to the machines for longwall working, others were introduced for room-and-pillar conditions. By 1955, Lansdown felt that trials had gone on long enough to justify a far greater rate of face mechanisation based on well-proved machines. There were mechanisation staff at all levels and area mechanisation teams to supervise installing equipment on the face, bringing it up to full capacity, training the team at the face and staying with the installation until it had achieved its intended satisfactory results. A wide range of training courses were available ranging up to a three-year course of directed practical training for engineers entering with university degrees or Higher National Certificate.

The safety record, where I have earlier quoted the great improvements in the rates for death and serious injury, was marred by an increase in the total injury figures. The distinction drawn in official records is between the more serious category 'reportably injured' (as defined in Chapter 4, page 61), and 'total injuries' comprising both reportably injured and others which cause at least three days' absence from work. Sir Harold Roberts, then Chief Inspector of Mines, acknowledged the great achievements of the Board over its period of stewardship, but was critical of the rate for these accidents which represented one a year for every three workers in the industry. The inspector did grant that these figures might be 'affected by social and economic factors and therefore are not a reliable measure of safety conditions' (in plain English meaning that under the old regime men with lesser injuries stayed on at work for fear of losing income but now had improved State sickness benefits), but pointed out that factories had been able to avoid similar increases in the lesser injuries.

By this time, the industry had 300 state registered nurses in its medical service, with 2,000 medical room attendants (half of them full-time), a network of medical officers and

346 medical centres. Mention health in the context of coal-winning, and the predictable, very understandable, reaction of most people is to ask about effects of dust, particularly pneumoconiosis, the most serious occupational disease of mineworkers. Inhaling excessive amounts of dust may cause changes in the lung. They may be simple, consisting of small aggregations of dust with fibrous tissue appearing in the lung substance. But they may also be complicated. In that case there is a background of simple pneumoconiosis with further large masses of fibrous tissue, generally thought to be due to additional effects of tuberculous infection. The Board set up a large-scale pneumoconiosis field research project by its Chief Medical Officer, Dr J. M. Rogan, in these terms:

> To determine how much and what kinds of dust cause pneumoconiosis and to establish what environmental conditions should be maintained if mineworkers are not to be disabled by dust that they breathe during the course of their work.

In collaboration with the NUM, the Ministry of Fuel and Power and the Medical Research Council, the Board planned the project to extend for ten years, based principally on twenty-five pits with dust covering the complete range of quantity and quality encountered in British mines. Everyone in the pits was examined by X-ray every $3\frac{1}{2}$ years and the dust concentrations measured. First findings included the feature that the extent of certification was unreliable as an index of the true prevalence of the disease; it was more a reflection of the local awareness among the men. With better examinations in the future, the medical staff expected the rate of certification to rise until the whole mining population had been examined – as a result not of an increase in true incidence, but of more discovery of the disease. The true prevalence was thought to be falling because of improved dust suppression. Other investigations dealt with 'beat disease' – the inflammation of the joints in knee, elbow, wrist or hand – nystagmus (considerably reduced as underground lighting improved), rheumatism, dermatitis, the rare but sometimes fatal Weil's Disease characterised by jaundice and pains in the muscles, and epidermophytosis. Oddly, the last disease named, better known as fungus infection of the skin of the feet, seemed to have been aggravated by the wider availability of pithead baths. Experiments were started with fungicides.

Research on coal processing – centred on a research station near Cheltenham under Dr J. Bronowski – was stated by the Director-General of Research, Dr R. W. Idris Jones, to be determined by four contemporary features:

1   the general shortage of coal and the deterioration in its quality in the seams from which it was drawn;
2   the introduction of mining methods resulting in producing an increasing proportion of small coal;
3   increasing demand by the carbonisation industries for coal that they could process by established methods, and the need to rely increasingly for other purposes on low-rank non-caking coals;
4   The clean-air legislation which would require large quantities of ordinary bituminous coal to be replaced by solid smokeless fuels.

At that time the coke and gas industries were big and selective users of coals that had to meet their requirements in terms of ash, sulphur and 'caking property' – that is the capability of yielding a strong coke; these needs were set most severely by the manufacturers of coke for metallurgical purposes. But the large part of the country's coal reserves were coals of what are called lower ranks which produce only weak coke or even non-coherent powder when carbonised (that is, heated in the absence of air to yield gas, coke and a range of liquid products). This affected both the carbonisation industries and the prospects for making a smokeless fuel for domestic use. The main objectives consequently became to establish new methods of producing smokeless fuels from weakly-caking coals which were not in demand by the coke and gas industries, and also to develop a scientific understanding of blending coals for carbonisation. This would enable the carbonisation industries to 'extend' the quantities of the higher quality coking and gas coals by blending with them others of slightly lesser quality while still meeting the criteria of the specifications for the quality of, particularly, the coke. Only a small proportion of the coal output was directly 'smokeless' (as defined by the Committee on Air Pollution known as the Beaver Committee) – such as anthracite and the Welsh steam coals – and the rest would need to be processed for smokeless burning in domestic grates. Alternatively, the domestic grates would need to be improved to ensure that ordinary coals could be burnt without making smoke. There were already small outputs of manufactured fuels, in addition to gas coke, but they tended to be based on one source of coal; the processes needed to be investigated to extend the scope of the coals that could be used in them. For dealing with the small coal which was of low financial value, briquetting processes of several kinds were examined, some ingeniously based on new techniques of compressing the coal powder without adding any binder to hold them together.

Within the scientific organisations primarily set up for scientific control over the operations of the industry, there were also a number of research projects. Some were 'internal', such as the projects on improving the accuracy and speed of chemical analyses of coal for the basic properties and for trace components when these were of special interest; examples were fluorine, thought to be damaging pastures, and germanium for use in transistors and allied electronic devices. Others were more directly related to production needs. For example, the Coal Survey Organisation investigated the use of microflora (fossilised tiny plants) as a means of correlating coal seams, that is identifying the coal found in samples obtained by exploratory drilling (known as 'cores') in relation to those found in cores from other drillings elsewhere. This was of great importance in production planning, enabling the production engineers to gain a true picture of the depth, thickness and extent of seams as well as their quality. Research was in progress to render non-polluting the effluents from coke ovens and also discharged mine-waters. Scientific detection in advance of the beginnings of mine fires and heatings made progress as an aid to safety.

Operational research teams, known as the Field Investigation Group, supplied detailed reports to the Production Department with data on efficiency including true costs of such activities as underground haulage and conveying, tunnel and roadway construction, underground communications and methods of roof support.

To make available the technical information obtained in its various activities, the Board issued Information Bulletins, reports, papers, handbooks, training manuals, Codes of Rules and NCB Specifications. Today, this may seem a normal enough type of activity for a large, progressive organisation whether publicly or privately-owned. Yet, as mentioned in Chapter 4, this was acknowledged by technical men dealing with the industry as a major change with great attendant benefits, from the secrecy and inadequate technical service characteristic of the privately-owned pits. Supplementing all this in-house activity, the Board also sponsored many relevant projects in outside organisations. For the applied research into both domestic equipment and industrial plant using coal, the main agency was the British Coal Utilisation Research Association. Fundamental work was placed in universities, including a programme on the fundamental structure of coal at the Cavendish Laboratory at Cambridge.

After a detailed survey of carbonisation plants – largely small ones producing cokes of very variable quality – the Board had drawn up a comprehensive programme for reconstructing some of them and building completely new ones, planned to carbonise at least 1,000 tons a day to minimise operating and capital costs. This side of the Board's activities had been criticised by the Fleck Committee as seriously under strength. Higher status was recommended for carbonisation directors in the four main carbonising divisions (South-Western, East Midlands, North-Eastern and Durham), with general strengthening of technical staff and properly organised constructional and chemical engineering branches at headquarters. This was one of the recommendations that was not accepted without question. The Board agreed to strengthen the department at headquarters but, in its statement of reactions to the Fleck Report, reported itself as 'still considering' appointing divisional directors. Later it decided to appoint two such divisional carbonisation directors. In 1956 the Clean Air Act had been passed so that local authorities became authorised to create smoke control areas. Until the results of researches into new smokeless fuels could be seen as products on the markets (or until improved coal-burning appliances became available), the Board foresaw that large additional quantities of smokeless fuel might be demanded and that these would have to be improved cokes made by existing carbonisation equipment. Dr R. J. Morley, the Director-General of Carbonisation at headquarters, referred to these demands, and the work under way to meet them, as 'certain to present new opportunities and new responsibilities to the Board in their capacity as the processors of the raw coal which they produce'.

PEOPLE

How much progress was made in transforming the attitudes of understandably rebellious men whose views had been formed in a period of often harsh struggles against owners who sometimes waxed fat but themselves suffered from time to time owing to shrinking markets and falling prices? In a somewhat qualified report on achievements, Mr W. H. Sales, at one time member of the national board, then appointed Chairman of North-Eastern Division from February 1957, summarised the background before power-loading in down-to-earth terms. Commenting on the nature of the work and the difficulty of the job before the Board, he observed:

> As practical men, we must realise how difficult it is to make a man enthuse about throwing 12 or more tons of coal a distance of seven feet or so, in about 6 hours of working time, often in dust-laden, warm, humid atmospheres, and in cramped positions – and keep this up daily for 40 years or more.

One important index of the Board's success has been quoted earlier – the sharply reduced ratio of days lost in disputes in coal-mining compared with those lost in other industries.

In fact, the absolute number of working days lost per year in mining in the period 1947–55 was lower than the average for any earlier period except 1927–9 when the whole industry was licking its wounds after the enormously damaging national stoppage of 1926.

Sales acknowledged an element of good fortune in the recent performance as well as any change due to new relationships in a nationalised industry. For the period had been one of full employment, rising welfare standards and rising living standards – therefore broadly one of reduced social stress and a more congenial economic and social environment. And yet within this environment a new type of dispute had developed. Instead of massive union-led strikes there were more smaller disputes. These breakdowns in human relations appeared to include strikes against the management and also some against the authority of the union. Some of the continuing difficulties were attributed to such features as these:

1 Coalmining is highly localised; consequently tensions and problems arising within the community may be reflected at work;
2 The strong sense of community insulates miners to some extent from pressures of general public opinion;
3 At work, miners depend very greatly on one another for production and for safety so that their very lives rest on the co-operation, goodwill and even self-sacrifice of their fellows; this results in an exceptionally close-knit sense of group identity with consequences of strength but also of higher tensions;
4 Within the community, there is a strong sense of tradition, which may become conservatism preserving customs and practices as traditions without critical thought about their validity or value.

A further possible factor, mentioned by Sales, was that 'the unity of trade union leadership and trade union rank and file, nurtured in the past by a common experience of struggle', was possibly being weakened or endangered. Rightly, though ironically, in view of later developments, he saw the central need of the industry as a policy of 'emotional security'.

Fig. 5 A housing estate at Ladywood, North-Eastern Division, built for miners in the mid-1950s by the Coal Industry Housing Association. (NCB.)

Meanwhile, the Board had also set up in 1952 a Coal Industry Housing Association (CIHA) which had built some 20,000 houses during the following four years in areas where more houses were needed for miners than the local authorities could provide. (Fig. 5). Since they were let at the same rents as the local authority houses, they cost the Board about £1 million a year. But they were nevertheless needed if the highly productive coalfields, notably in the East and West Midlands, were not to be left short of men. Consequently further building by CIHA continued to be approved by the Board.

What were the official union reactions? Naturally, the then president of the NUM, Mr W. E. Jones, asserted that the success of nationalisation would be judged by its ability to deal with the problems of reconstruction and general efficiency 'and by the extent to which there is a progressive improvement in the working and living conditions of those employed therein'. But he also paid tribute to the great change in the employer–worker relationship which was 'nowhere more clearly brought out than in the sphere of consultation'. Joint discussions at the National Consultative Council had had an impact on the general plans of the Board that could not be over-estimated. Little wonder that Mr Jones also went on to comment:

> Having demanded nationalisation, and secured it, the union has a responsibility for ensuring . . . success. It is in this field especially that the standards of well-being of its members in the industry, and their families, can be extended.
>
> We have determined that the union must remain independent so that it can properly carry out its function as a union – nevertheless, the union believes that the basic problems confronting the industry can only be solved if there is the fullest collaboration with those who, because of their experience in the industry, have a real contribution to make.

So the policy was reasoned collaboration but no automatic sycophancy. And Emanuel Shinwell, pilot of the nationalisation measure through the Commons, when asked to look back and assess, also felt encouraged and reasonably happy at the outcome, even though he admitted that ten years of nationalisation had failed to remove all the difficulties. For he saw among the 'manifold advantages' of nationalisation that they had:

> secured for the whole nation the ownership and control of our greatest industrial asset . . . replaced unbridled competition . . . by unified administration and co-operation . . . raised the status of those who are employed in the industry

. . . . Our mining communities are now beginning to be enriched by welfare arrangements, the townships throughout the coalfields are less squalid than they were. The mineworkers are relatively better off in material things . . . more friendly disposition among those responsible for management, to which the mineworker, because he is not one who will bear malice, will respond.

GENERAL ACHIEVEMENTS

So at the end of the first decade all seemed set fair. When the Annual Report for 1956 was published, the press criticised a proposed coal price increase announced simultaneously (some had the grace to admit that this still left British coal the cheapest in Europe); this apart, reluctantly, they granted that the report was the best yet. The *Daily Telegraph,* for example, a stern foe of nationalisation, thought Mr Bowman a little too optimistic, while admitting 'He has certainly some reason to be pleased at the emergence of the industry, under his auspices, from its protracted teething troubles'. Metaphorically wagging a finger at the miners (as ever!), it exhorted them to maintain the better spirit cited by Bowman, adding gratuitously: 'The miners need have no fear that theirs is a dying industry'.

It was not a situation wholly without troubles. But productivity was the highest in Europe, power-loading was being rapidly introduced, major reconstruction schemes were shortly due to be completed, much of the poison had been drained from human relations in the industry, and demand for energy was increasing and forecast to continue to increase. Then, as though in a classical drama, at this moment of great promise there arose a cloud on the horizon no larger than a fall in coal demand of $2\frac{1}{2}$ per cent. It was a portent of far greater blows to come.

SUGGESTED FURTHER READING

National Coal Board, *Annual Reports and Statements of Account* for the individual years ending 31 December 1947 to 1957 inclusive

National Coal Board. The first ten years. Edited by Sir Guy Nott-Bower and R. H. Walkerdine. (*Colliery Guardian* [undated but presumably 1957])

Sir Harold Hartley. *Europe's Growing Needs of Energy – How can they be met?* (Organisation for European Economic Co-operation, 1956)

Plan for Coal (National Coal Board, 1950)

Investing in Coal (National Coal Board, 1956)

National Coal Board. *Report of the Advisory Committee on Organisation.* (National Coal Board, 1955) – known as the Fleck Report

Press comments on NCB *Annual Report,* 6 June 1957

CHAPTER 7

The great turnabout

Tempora mutantur (times change)

anonymous

The 1957 Annual Report unfortunately gives the distinct impression that the Board had not yet realised what was beginning to hit it. In 1956 inland coal consumption reached a peak for the post-war period of 218·4 million tons; the following year it had fallen to 213·2 million tons. The Board explained this fall as due to exceptional circumstances – an increased average temperature accounting for 3 million tons of the fall, some check to growth of industrial production, more efficient use of coal and the increased use of oil. Nevertheless it was noted that oil equivalent to 16·5 million tons of coal was used during the year 'in markets where it was an alternative to coal'.

Assessing what had happened to exports was probably more difficult, for during 1955 it had proved necessary to import as much coal as had been exported. The Board, with the approval of the government, therefore decided to reduce exports. But the demands of contracts meant that this reduction only took effect in 1956 and 1957. During the latter year attempts were again made to sell abroad some of the extra tonnages that had become available as a result of the drop in inland use. The failure of these efforts was attributed to the same factors as those operating in Britain, but also understandably to the fact that prospective customers had often by now made long-term contracts with other suppliers. Discussing these trends, the NCB added hopefully: 'the fall does not of course mean that demand has reached its peak . . . inland

demand for coal is expected to increase in the future'. Ironically, despite the fall in general market demand, the Board
actually had to import large coal – mainly from the USA –
and sell it to meet requirements at a loss. (The inadequate
supply of large coal received urgent attention, particularly
in 1957, in several different ways, though within a few years
one of the main users – the railways – had dropped their
demand from over 11 million tons a year to virtually nothing
as they turned from steam locomotives to diesel and diesel
electric.)

At the end of 1957 and for the following five months or
so the industry had the attention of the first major enquiry
into the workings of a large nationalised industry by a Select
Committee of the House of Commons. During this intensive
grilling of all its senior members, including the Chairman,
Sir James Bowman – over 900 questions were listed and a
series of detailed memoranda were submitted by the Board –
the NCB did discuss rather more fully the threat from the
competition of oil. It reported a switch in emphasis in its
operations to the reduction costs as against the absolute
priority given earlier to volume of production. The Committee
appointed by the Conservative Government under the chairmanship of Sir Toby Low was critical of the advance planning
of the 1949 plan, which it thought a failure; it thought that
even the 1956 plan *Investing in Coal* was 'already in jeopardy'
and wanted the Ministry of Power (as it then was) to make
greater financial checks on investment schemes. The final
report acknowledged the financial burdens imposed on the
Board by its statutory duty to consult the minister before
raising prices, by its being banned from exporting at much
higher prices until the home market was satisfied, and by its
being compelled to import and re-sell at a loss (that is, instead
of leaving users to import for themselves at the best prices
they could obtain). A later Board Chairman quoted the loss
falling on the Board for this reason as adding up to no less
than £70 million. (In the early years, the shortage of home
supplies had been aggravated by the demands of Ernest
Bevin's foreign policy. Bevin wanted coal sent to Europe so
that he could act the strong man in four-power negotiations;

It was duly supplied, but Britain then had to buy in dearer coal for home needs as a consequence of Bevin's delusions of grandeur, though the losses were not, of course, charged to the Foreign Office.)

The Chairman and other senior officers were closely questioned on the investment made in pits producing coal at a loss, but the Committee accepted the logic that led to this situation – bizarre in normal commercial terms. For in some cases it had proved necessary in order to maintain the skilled labour force or because the particular coal was in especial demand, such as anthracite or coking coal. Rightly the Commons Committee commented that as the demand for coal dropped there was a greater incentive to close the pits producing the more expensive coal – and it added reservations about methods of doing this which showed proper social concern. Yet while it recognised the great difficulty of judging the efficiency of individual pits by any single criterion in view of the variability of natural conditions (as the Fleck Committee had found earlier), the Commons Committee deliberately turned aside from an exercise that might well have been very informative and rewarding for the industry as a whole. It was 'conscious of the absence of a yardstick by which to judge the performance of the Board'. It found comparisons with the performance of the industry before nationalisation of doubtful value because 'circumstances had changed so much' – a strange comment since the aim of the exercise would have been precisely to determine the result of that very change in circumstances. And the final blindfold the Committee chose to adopt for itself was summarised in these words :

> To have sought independent evidence either on the performance of previously privately-owned mines in the United Kingdom, or on the progress and conditions in coal industries in other countries would, in Your Committee's opinion, have taken them far beyond their proper function.

Since the Committee's function had been defined in the vaguest terms (. . . to examine the Reports and Accounts of the Nationalised Industries . . .') there must in fact have been other reasons, not disclosed. However, on a central question before the industry – the essential character of the trends in consumption – the Committee appeared to accept the Board's estimate that this was a 'dip in the curve' needing short-term measures while the long-term plan remained unchanged.

In fact, the fall in consumption – both inland and export – continued in Britain, Belgium, France, Germany and Holland. But the Board continued to think in terms of maintaining the productive capacity of the industry, refraining from large-scale closures (though closing fifty-three pits on technical and economic grounds), controlling recruitment, and cutting open-cast production at great cost in lost profit to cushion the effect of falling consumption on the deep mines. Fresh consultations with the main groups of consumers with detailed discussions of forward trends led to a further revision of plans, published as *Revised Plan for Coal*. Scaling down the estimates of 230 million tons a year from deep-mined and a further 10 from opencast production in 1965, the new totals were seen as between 190 and 205 million tons inland consumption at that time with a further 10 million exported. The Board appeared to be encouraged by the conclusion that even the lower end of the range of total demand – at 200 million tons a year – was a little higher than the then current levels. The grand total was built up of expected increased use of coal for generating electricity and for making coke; other users such as the gas industry and railways would take less. To meet it, output would be raised in North-Eastern, East Midlands, West Midlands and South-Western divisions while Scottish division would be left at the same level and the others reduced. The revision was set in the framework of aiming towards increasing productive efficiency, closing by 1965 up to 400 of the original collieries taken over. Plans were to be discussed with government departments so that they could arrange to attract other industries to areas where men could not be offered reasonable alternative employment. The aim briefly was that by 1965, the coal industry will be more compact, more efficient, and better able to compete with alternative fuels, with 80 per cent of its output coming from new and reconstructed collieries. The industry will not expand to the size that was originally expected, but with an annual output of 200 million tons or more in 1965, and for many years after, it will still make by far the biggest contribution to the country's fuel requirements.

In 1960 there was a marked upsurge in demand, bringing it into line with the estimates in the revised plan, promoting hopes that 1961 would remain at the same level given steady industrial activity and normal temperatures, obscuring the true disastrous decline that was developing, and leading to assessments that the Board's selling activities and improved consumer service were helping to maintain a high level of demand in the face of stronger competition. But between the end of 1956 and the end of 1959 the total consumption had fallen no less than 33 million tons a year; the recovery in 1960 accounted for about 8 million tons.

FIGHTING FOR MARKETS

The industry had indeed run a vigorous marketing campaign. In 1959 the NCB greatly expanded the technical and commercial sales service advising industrial consumers, helping them in assessing plant performance. It also contributed strongly to the National Industrial Fuel Efficiency Service and to the Coal Utilisation Council. To combat competitive sales propaganda that coal was 'old-fashioned', it also published an illustrated booklet, *The Case for Coal;* distributed widely to industrialists, architects, consulting engineers and others involved in decisions on fuel, it showed that modern techniques enabled coal to be burnt smokelessly, economically and with the minimum of handling. To snatch the initiative from the main competitor the theme constantly hammered in the booklet and in extensive press advertising was 'progressive industry is going forward on coal'. At many collieries the coal-burning plants were used to demonstrate how efficiently and conveniently coal could be burnt in modernised equipment. In co-operation with a finance house, a loan scheme was introduced, known as the 'Housewarming Plan', encouraging householders to install central heating and other modern coal-burning appliances which would burn a wide range of fuels while meeting the needs of the Clean Air Act. This received a good response.

Almost £5 million was spent on research and development in 1960. At the British Coal Utilisation Research Association (BCURA), heavily supported by the Board, preliminary trials began of a fully automatic industrial boiler plant; the objective was to develop machinery that would work automatically for long periods, burning coal at high efficiency emitting no smoke or grit. BCURA had also designed an automatically controlled miniature chain grate stoker suitable for blocks of flats. After successful trials two further units were prepared for installation by the winter of 1960–1. Broadly, the emphasis was on improving both the handling of coal on consumers' premises and the disposal of ash. Pilot plants were built to assess the commercial possibilities of two processes for making premium smokeless fuels. One in the West Midlands converted what are known as 'high volatile' coals – which would normally burn in household grates generating a large amount of smoke – into a 'char' by the advanced technique of carbonising in a fluid bed. The fine coal is kept in motion by gas passing through it so that it behaves as a fluid. The char is then briquetted hot. The other plant in South-Western division took anthracite fines ('duff') which were difficult to burn, blended them with low volatile coals, stuck them together with pitch and mildly heated them, yielding a high-quality smokeless fuel. At an earlier stage of development was a further process for making from anthracite duff briquettes for domestic central heating and cookers. Other researches progressed on plant for producing gas from low-grade coal.

During 1959, the Minister of Power had also set up two committees on highly relevant topics. One, chaired by Mr N. M. Peech, on solid smokeless fuels, concluded that demand in people's homes would increase from 6 million tons at that time to almost double by 1965 but that producers' tentative plans should balance supply with demand by the end of that six-year period. For the closed and openable stoves there were ample supplies, and also for the improved open grates. The only conceivable problem the committee saw was for supplies for what it called the 'unimproved open grate', that is the older types with a shallow fire-bed which needed more reactive, though still smokeless fuels; but even here it estimated that demand would probably be met.

The other special committee, chaired by Sir Alan Wilson, reviewed work on developing processes for making derivatives from coal – products to be sold as chemicals or as liquid or gaseous fuels. Carbonisation was seen as continuing to be the most important method of processing coal in Britain. Far from recommending new methods for stepping up chemical production, the committee found that chemicals that could be extracted from crude benzole and tar were present in greater quantities than were then required by the chemical industry. To expand the production of gas it looked to the Lurgi process; this was a German-designed process which made gas from coal without also making coke and thus gave great flexibility, since the demands for the two fuels did not always go hand in hand. The Lurgi process also took non-caking coals. In fact, the Gas Boards did complete a Lurgi plant, at Westfield in Fife, in 1960 and a further one at Coleshill in Warwickshire shortly afterwards. The NCB collaborated with them in various ways in respect of testing coals for suitability and arranging coal supplies. The process proved to make gas that was more expensive than that later available from petroleum sources and then the North Sea. The Coleshill plant was closed down but that at Westfield, now modified, is actively in use – sponsored by American interests – for developing processes for making substitute natural gas from coal.

On another front – turning a potential hazard into an asset – over a third of the methane drained from collieries to improve their safety was used as fuel either directly at collieries or by selling it to the gas industry. By the end of 1961 no fewer than ninety-five installations were operating, selling almost 3,300 million cubic feet of the gas during the

year. Schemes were prepared to extend the practice of draining and using the methane, in some cases for firing the coke
ovens associated with the collieries.

Meanwhile great technical progress had been made in
winning the coal. By 1961 almost all the coal was mechanically
cut, half was power-loaded from the cutter straight on to the
conveyor, and almost all was mechanically conveyed. After
the relative stagnation in output per manshift mentioned
earlier as a feature of the second five-year period, productivity
rose from 24·9 cwt per manshift in 1957 to 28·9 in 1961;
for faceworkers the corresponding figures were 69·3 rising to
83·5. The average horsepower of electric motors in use per
man went up over the same period by about a third so that,
viewed in the reciprocal direction, the average number of
manshifts that had to be worked to obtain every thousand
tons of deep-mined saleable coal had also improved. At
nationalisation this had required over 900 manshifts, then
the number levelled off around 800 for several years, but
from 1957 onwards ever fewer manshifts were needed and in
1961 this index was below 700. And although costs
increased, it had proved to be possible to obtain higher prices,
so that collieries were still making operating profits during
this period, before the charging of the interest they were
compelled to pay transformed the consolidated financial
results into a loss. (At this stage, incidentally, in common with
other nationalised industries, coal came under pressure by
the government to accept its obligation to achieve surpluses
of sufficient magnitude to cover its deficits over a five-year
period, allowing for interest and depreciation and making
provision for allocations to reserves as a contribution to capital
development.)

Despite these various pressures, the Board in its 1961 report
felt able to state confidently:

The British coal industry entered 1962 more efficient and
better organised to meet the challenge of competition than
ever before. The Board will press forward energetically
with their sales promotion campaigns . . . the aim is to meet
the expected future demand for coal at the lowest practic-

able cost, and in particular to provide British industry with coal as cheap as, or cheaper than, that available to its foreign competitors. . . . The spirit of the industry, in the face of a tremendous challenge of changing circumstances, is excellent.

Yet in 1961 the fall in consumption, apparently arrested the previous year, had been resumed. A breakdown by classes of users showed growth only in the demand by power stations. All other classes of user took smaller quantities, the biggest decline being in the offtake by the railways who took one-seventh less in 1961 than in the preceding year, continuing a fall that had already been going on for more than a decade. Overall, this was a pattern that was to continue for some years. Behind the new situation of 'fierce competition for the Board's markets' (explicitly acknowledged in the 1961 Report) was a marked and decisive shift in the price relationship between oil and coal.

As Table 11 shows, oil gently, though erratically, became cheaper; coal, also a little erratically, became rather dearer. Both features worked in the same direction to alter the price relationship in favour of oil. Considering fuel supplies for generating electricity and comparing them in terms of pence per therm (including the tax, in the case of oil, for 1961), the ratio of the cost of heat supplied by oil divided by that coming from coal slid from 1·33 in 1955 to unity four years later; in 1960 oil actually became cheaper (until the situation was redressed by the imposition of the tax in the following

Table 11   *Fuel for power stations*

Year	Pence per therm		Coal price/oil price A/B	Oil price/coal price B/A
	Coal (A)	Oil (B)		
1955	1·5	2·0	0·75	1·33
1956	1·7	1·9	0·89	1·12
1957	1·7	2·0	0·85	1·18
1958	1·8	1·8	1·00	1·00
1959	1·7	1·7	1·00	1·00
1960	1·7	1·6	1·06	0·94
1961	1·7	1·9*	0·89	1·12

* a tax of 2*d.* a gallon was imposed on fuel oil in 1961.
All prices are in old pence, *d.*

year). Before this stage, oil's advantages of higher calorific value per unit weight, easier handling as a liquid – meaning also cheaper handling in industry – and negligible ash content had had to be offset against its greater cost per unit of heat supplied. When coal lost its price advantage, then in straight commercial terms the writing was truly on the wall for the industry.

The ratio of prices has understandably proved to be a most significant index. The trend in coal consumption follows it, not perfectly but as a strong general tendency. And despite some fluctuations in the early 1960s, that trend continued downward in both the ratio and the demand for coal (from 1957) for many years.

The exercise is carried back only to 1955 because oil-fired stations were of little significance before that date. And although other detailed factors would enter into the prices paid by individual factories in industry, the relationship is a good guide to that of prices for general industry too. Behind the brief halt in the decline of oil prices in 1957 was the Suez crisis and its repercussions. By mid-November 1956 the Suez Canal was blocked by sunken ships, and tankers were being forced to make the longer run round the Cape of Good Hope, adding appreciably to transport costs in those days of much smaller tankers. Furthermore, in Britain oil supplies, as a precautionary measure, were restricted until May 1957.

The price of oil rose temporarily then continued to fall. The government – for reasons discussed in the following chapter – decided to give some degree of protection to the coal industry. The use of oil at power stations had increased from 7 million tons coal equivalent in 1959 to over 9 million some three years later; the electricity industry was asked to stop the switch from coal to oil. The government also refused licences for importing American coal and, in 1961, placed a duty of 2d. a gallon on oil used for burning, equivalent to 23s. 0d. per ton of coal used for steam-raising – for revenue reasons, it said, but taking into account the protective effect on coal. The introduction of nuclear energy for generating electricity – seen at its introduction largely as a means of supplementing coal supplies and even easing the pressure of demand for coal – now began to loom as a further threat, adding to the anxieties produced by the advances of oil into markets hitherto fuelled by coal. In 1955 an initial programme was adopted for constructing up to 2,000 megawatts of nuclear power stations, and this had been greatly expanded in 1957 to a nuclear programme of up to 6,000 megawatts capacity by 1965. The development of this programme soon became a highly contentious issue.

HUMAN PROBLEMS

From the great turning-point in 1957 the total manpower employed in the industry fell rapidly. In the first stage the board had, as mentioned earlier, controlled recruitment, reduced imports, reduced opencast working – and also stopped Saturday working. The colliery closures resulted largely in men being re-deployed into collieries that continued to operate; of 10,000 men in collieries closed or merged in 1961, only 100 remained unemployed a few months later. Yet overall the number of men was reduced from 704,000 on the books in 1957 to 571,000 some four years later.

Analysis of the reported figures suggests that the rundown was carried through with a minimum of serious disturbance for the men affected. Excluding transfers between collieries, the pits lost over 74,000 men in 1961 (while recruiting over 52,000 when and where they were needed so that the net reduction was nearly 22,000). But only some 3,000 represented dismissals and redundancies. Most of the remainder left – in the ugly official phrase – 'as a result of normal wastage', going to jobs in other industries.

Strangely, there was a steady increase in the percentage absence from work during the time from 1954 to 1961 which went on during both the expanding phase and the contracting one. An attempt to pinpoint the reasons by a research team led by Dr R. B. Buzzard of the Medical Research Council – seconded to the NCB for this purpose – and Mr F. D. K. Liddell, the Head of the Board's Medical Statistics Branch, led to rather uncertain conclusions. The investigation was sponsored by the Board and carried out with the agreement of both the NUM and the National Association of Colliery Overmen, Deputies and Shotfirers. As Dr Buzzard acknowledges, the subject of attendance among miners has always been controversial; that was the point of inviting a man from the MRC rather than leaving it to a wholly internal team. But this tactic did not exorcise the contentiousness of the subject. The original report was completed in 1958 but not published for five years; during that time there had evidently been some running battles to judge by the terse disclaimer that takes the place of the more unusual gushing appreciation in the preface to the report.

> The National Coal Board take no responsibility . . . reservations . . . disappointed that the authors have not committed themselves . . . the hypotheses put forward . . . do not give a sufficient explanation of the steady increase in percentage absence from 1954 to 1961.

In a nutshell, the investigators opened by apparently querying the premise, since the statistics of absence and attendance did not provide sufficient information; they found enormous variability between and within occupations, faces, collieries, areas, divisions. Then their disturbing conclusions were that 'neither alterations to wage scales nor incentives to good attendance nor disciplinary measures can be shown to have had any sustained effect in altering' the average number of shifts that miners worked. The hypothesis that they felt to be capable of explaining most of the phenomena they discovered was 'that a natural balance tends to be maintained between efforts, attendance and length of working life, in which alterations to one would lead to compensating alterations in the others'. From this they argued that the use of incentives or deterrents to improve attendance would give only spurious benefits in amount of work done; major and sustained increases in attendance were only likely to be achieved by measures reducing the effort of work in the more arduous occupations, improved training to enable it to be done with greater physical efficiency, or improved selection.

My own impression would be that physical effort had in

fact been reduced by mechanisation, even though conditions of work remained more unpleasant and more strenuous than in other industries, so that this hypothesis should lead to the expectation of improved attendance. In its own reports the Board commented that there were good reasons why absence rates might be higher in mining than in some other industries; accident and sickness rates were higher and often the cycle of operations meant that a man late for a shift could not get down because coal was being wound. So, without much success, it continued to seek the help of the NUM to combat absenteeism and raised the matter at consultative bodies at all levels.

Happily, the death rate continued to fall; 1961 saw the lowest number of deaths ever recorded by the Board – though still representing the sacrifice of 234 lives. Yet the general and serious accident rate remained unsatisfactory, leading to a decision to run a National Safety Year drawing in the 'consultative machinery' as well as using exhibitions, competitions, training courses, films and booklets as part of a wide-ranging campaign.

Research on suppressing dust had shown that on coal-cutting machines the best results were obtained by flushing with water the cutting surfaces of the picks that directly cut into the coal, wetting the dust at the point where it was generated. To the end of 1961 over a quarter of a million men had been examined in the periodic X-ray scheme for the control of pneumoconiosis, helping to focus attention on those collieries demanding particular attention to suppressing dust. The prevalence of the disease – over 13 per cent of men were found to have it in some degree and about 1 per cent had 'progressive massive fibrosis' – was taken as reflecting many past years of exposure to dust conditions. The field research, mentioned earlier, continued in order to determine the amounts and types of coal dust causing this disease, while the Board supported MRC work on long-term trials of treatments for the more serious fibrosis.

By this time, too, there were 364 medical centres, most of them staffed with state registered nurses and supported with several times that number of full-time and part-time medical room attendants. Doctors were continuing the practice of checking new entrants to the industry and carrying out medical examinations for other purposes when necessary, as well as advising on the control of health hazards. Other research on the effects of hot and humid working conditions led to tentative recommendations on limits to be set – a feature of growing importance as coal was being won from greater depths.

Pithead baths served over 95 per cent of the mineworkers – with operating costs, incidentally, of £5½ million – and the Board made grants of about a million pounds a year to the Coal Industry Social Welfare Organisation which provides social welfare for families as well as miners. Hundreds more houses continued to go up under the supplementary building programme of the Coal Industry Housing Association.

At this critical phase in its battle for survival, the industry entered a new phase marked by the imprint of the flamboyant personality of Alfred Robens, appointed Deputy Chairman late in 1960 in order to become Chairman early in 1961. In his first year as Chairman he was created a life peer as Lord Robens of Woldingham. The flavour of his impact comes over very clearly from his own not over-modest account of his stewardship.

SUGGESTED FURTHER READING

National Coal Board, *Annual Reports and Statements of Account* for the individual years 1957 to 1961 inclusive
Revised Plan for Coal (National Coal Board, 1959)
Report from the Select Committee on Nationalised Industries (Reports and Accounts) (HMSO, 1958)
Report of the Committee on Solid Smokeless Fuels, Cmnd 999 (HMSO, 1960)
Report of the Committee on Coal Derivatives, Cmnd 1120 (HMSO, 1960)
The Financial and Economic Obligations of the Nationalised Industries, Cmnd 1337 (HMSO, 1961)
R. B. Buzzard and F. D. K. Liddell, *Coalminers' Attendance at Work* (National Coal Board, Medical Service, 1963)
Lord Robens, *Ten Year Stint* (Cassell, 1972)

CHAPTER 8

Fight for survival

Say not the struggle naught availeth,
The labour and the wounds are vain

Arthur Hugh Clough

For several reasons the new appointment led to uproar. Alfred Robens had been an official of the Union of Distributive and Allied Workers, then was elected Member of Parliament in the sweeping Labour victory of 1945. In the Labour government he held a junior ministerial post first at the Ministry of Transport, then from 1947 to 1951 at the Ministry of Fuel and Power. Later, for a few months, he was Minister of Labour. At the time when the news of his appointment as Chairman 'broke' he was a senior member of Labour's 'Shadow Cabinet' working closely with Hugh Gaitskell, then the party leader. Yet, bound by a pledge of secrecy given to Harold Macmillan (the Tory prime minister who had appointed him and wished himself to see Gaitskell first), Robens had not breathed a word to his close colleague. According to Robens's own account – 'facing a quietly angry Gaitskell' – this awkward situation was readily tidied up by a simple explanation of the facts. The difficulty had arisen because *The Guardian* had scooped the announcement, before all these behind-the-scenes negotiations had been completed; the controversies elsewhere caused much more furore. Within political circles, there were loudly critical comments from Labour MPs who thought the appointment a means of weakening Labour's leadership, while some Conservative MPs made equally angry attacks on the grounds that Robens had no practical experience of controlling a large-scale industry. Probably more seriously, it appeared to upset managers and men – though the two showed rather different emphases – of the coal industry itself. Robens quotes a letter to *The Times* by the President of the British Association of Colliery Management, Jim Bullock, in which he wrote :

> Management's criticism of the appointment is the appalling idea that in this industry there is no person capable of handling the business of this great, complex and complicated industry; but that someone from outside the industry with nowhere near the experience can do it better than those with a lifetime's experience.
>
> My union represents men of the highest skills and experience in the industry, men of high integrity and calibre, and this appointment comes as a distinct shock to all of them and makes nonsense of my union's efforts to establish an appointments procedure . . .

Among the mineworkers, the appointment followed a spate of rumours fed by speculative press comment that the Conservative government intended to direct the NCB to return to coalfield competition; there was said to be a 'secret plan' prepared for this style of decentralisation. The NUM had for many years regarded the old system of competition between coalfields as completely unacceptable since it could lead to unemployment for miners in the more expensive coalfields. The need for centralised administration to prevent this had been an important part of the NUM's case for nationalisation. Yet here, after the battle had apparently been won, there appeared to be a risk of a return to earlier hated practices. In June 1960, the executive committee of the NUM unanimously passed a resolution declaring that 'any attempt by the Tory Government to interfere with the national structure of the coal mining industry by decentralisation . . . will be resisted by the NUM with every legitimate means at its disposal'. E. Jones, acting president, and Will Paynter, the general secretary, explained that they suspected this possibility because of documents, agitation by Conservative backbenchers, and the fact that the government had already decentralised the electricity industry.

Whether the suspicious were justified and the vigorous reaction led to a retreat or whether there had been an over-suspicious reaction to an insignificant movement among Conservative MPs, it is impossible to tell. But certainly on the same day, Richard Wood, Minister of Power, denied political motives behind Robens's appointment, referred to miners' fears of a 'dismantling' of the coal industry, and gave undertakings that there would be no denationalisation, that he sought to make the nationalised industry efficient, and that any changes proposed would be discussed with the Chairman and the Board.

Robens added his own assurances that there would be no decentralisation on broad policies like centrally negotiated wages. But he added that he thought it sensible to devolve authority on organisation 'to keep the command as near as possible to the point of production, so that the men who work in the industry know where to go for final decisions'. During and following his own induction period as Deputy Chairman, visiting coalfields and having discussions with personnel at every level, Robens evolved an opening policy which might be summarised under these heads:

1 The Board needed a massive sales campaign;
2 This in turn needed to be backed by the greatest mechanisation drive the industry had ever seen, with goodwill on the part of the men;
3 With this was needed a complete administrative reorganisation with greater authority for management levels below headquarters, but with no escape from personal responsibility;
4 They would not be handmaidens of the Civil Service. On this issue he specified that the Board would act commercially and would not tolerate any interference from the Government. If the Minister wanted to give the Board a directive, then it would have to be a statutory one under the Act, for publication in the Annual Report, so that the distinction between purely commercial decisions and political decisions could be clearly seen.

Recalling the whole period, Robens wrote: 'We never did have a directive of any kind'.

Setting out to build aggressive confidence and restore morale in an industry obviously shaken by the contraction of sales and manpower, Robens extensively involved himself in strong campaigns of high-powered selling, to show the people in the industry, as he put it, 'that the gaffer was quite prepared to get stuck in to try to win markets for our products'. More formally, the mood comes over in the review of the year in the Board's 1962 Report, when the new man had completed his second year of office.

> In 1962, productivity rose by nearly eight per cent, the tonnage lost through strikes and restrictions was almost halved and a financial surplus was made for the first time in six years.
> . . . Wider and more efficient use of machines resulted in 20,000 fewer men producing eight million more tons of coal from some 450 fewer coalfaces.
> . . . changing pattern of production. . . . A carefully planned recruitment policy helped to find alternative work within the industry for men no longer required. While many were found other jobs near their homes, the Board developed means of encouraging and helping men and their families to move . . . [to coalfields] where work was available . . . strengthening of partnership with the distributive trade and the appliance manufacturers . . . vigorous industrial sales campaign . . . 'Appproved Coal Merchants Scheme' was introduced to provide the domestic consumer with a much improved standard of service.
> The results achieved in 1962 have considerably strengthened the Board's ability to meet the tasks that lie ahead.

But despite all these very real achievements, including a fall in production costs due to the record increase in productivity – with every division throughout the country showing a creditable improvement – disposals of coal were down in almost every category except power stations. This continued the change in the pattern of coal consumption away from traditional markets for the higher-priced larger coals towards lower-priced small coals, aggravating the problems of the industry by resulting in a lower return for sales. The decline in demand for coal was only transiently arrested, though the total demand for energy continued to grow.

The general pattern of increases in the use of energy and a shift away from coal was not peculiar to Britain. In fact, Britain at that stage had retained a higher proportion of the energy market for coal than other West European countries. The 1965 White Paper (discussed below) said that the share taken by coal in 1964 in the four largest coal-producing countries in Western Europe was 49 per cent in West Germany, 44 per cent in France, 60 per cent in Belgium and 39 per cent in Holland; on a comparable basis the figure for Britain was 69 per cent. The West European Coal Producers with the NCB published a study in 1963 leading to the conclusions that on normal expectations of expansion of the world economy, a fuel shortage in ten to twenty years' time was more likely than a surplus. A temporary glut of oil had led to the relatively low level of oil prices. Costs would rise in the future because of the shortage and the increasing costs of prospecting and exploiting new oil deposits, and because the recently formed Organisation of Petroleum Exporting Countries covered more than nine-tenths of world exports of crude oil. 'These countries', added the report with reasonable prescience, 'might thus be tempted to increase their prices substantially.' Robens, in his book, quotes a very senior civil servant in the Ministry of Power as dismissing references to OPEC with the comment 'You can forget about them. They will never amount to a row of beans.'

The coal producers' study, referring to the inelasticity of fuel supply and demand, concluded its assessment of the world energy picture by warning:

If in the present circumstances it seems paradoxical to envisage a future rise in energy prices – and in oil prices in particular – such a rise is none the less inherent in the facts. At the moment, and perhaps for a little time to come, this contention arouses a certain degree of scepticism in uninformed circles . . . [Yet] such a development is inevitable.

As already quoted in the opening chapter, they concluded that future availability of European hard coal was essential for the safety and health of the European economy.

Backing up the campaign, Dr E. F. Schumacher, the NCB Economic Adviser (who is of German origin), mounted a lecture tour in West Germany in 1963 hammering at the theme of inevitable future oil shortages due to the limitations of nature and very probably the deliberate actions of man. He presented papers at international congresses and wrote frequently in German and British periodicals. Advocated by the coal producers was in essence that coal use should be directly subsidised, where it did not compete successfully with oil, on the grounds indicated above, plus the relative inflexibility of the coal industry so that it could not be switched on and off, and the basic strategic danger of depending on imports for a raw material so fundamental in so many aspects as fuel. The economic burden was estimated as possibly accumulating to one-tenth of 1 per cent of the GNP for the limited period in which oil was likely to remain cheaper than coal. For industries affected more seriously than the average, governments should apply 'special measures' – not spelt out in detail but implying extra subsidies for such areas as electricity, iron and steel, and cement, where fuel is a high part of costs.

Why were these arguments not accepted? Probing this question with senior officers of the present Department of Energy (the present form of the previous Ministry of Power), the answers I have received – withholding names at their owners' request – have included some based on personalia and others probably more fundamental. The former are, in essence, that Schumacher was not very highly regarded by his fellow economists in the government service and that in any case raising the money for a coal subsidy would mean increasing taxes and therefore adding to inflationary pressure. But basically I gather that Schumacher's argument was taken by officialdom as a partisan case put forward out of self-interest and not to be taken seriously as an objective analysis. Richard Marsh (who became minister in 1966) told me recently that at that time nobody outside the coal industry saw any future for coal and that the men at the ministry regarded some of the advocacy as hysterical. All the advice from all expert sources outside coal was that oil was plentiful, that oil prices would not rise as fast as those of coal, and that the future of oil supplies was secure. Robens in his book quotes his impression that around 1965–6 the idea that Britain should shed most of its coal industry with all its attendant problems, was widespread in the Civil Service. When he tried to persuade James Callaghan (at that time Chancellor of the Exchequer) to the contrary, the reply was 'I couldn't find an official in the whole of the Treasury who would accept your argument'.

FUEL POLICY 1965

When a Labour government was returned in 1964 (with a majority of only 5), committed to giving support to the coal industry and to developing a coherent fuel policy, it immediately put in hand a review and the following year published a White Paper. This gives the impression of resulting from a conflict between the political commitment to maintain the size of the coal industry – if necessary by protective measures – and departmental pressures in favour of a free market for fuel involving a free-for-all between the individual fuels. The reasons for protecting an indigenous industry – noted as being already part of the policies of the USA, France and the Federal Republic of Germany – were given in terms which can be summarised under these heads:

1 The coal industry saves imports.
2 Fullest economic use should be made of the large investment already made in it and the associated social investment.
3 Supplies to meet estimated demands were reasonably secure provided the industry was not disrupted by too sharp a decline.

4   Though oil was currently cheaper, the situation might change. Coal capacity once lost could be re-created only with difficulty.
5   There were practical limits to the rate at which the industry could contract economically.

Against these points were set the requirements not to carry protection to an extent that would make British fuel costs uncompetitive, and not to prevent the development of oil-refining in Britain; any aid should help the coal industry 'to bring about smoothly its transition to a more compact and competitive structure'. Protection consisted of retaining the 2*d.* a gallon tax on fuel oil, and the virtual ban on coal imports. Other forms of assistance were that the government would provide special funds to speed the closure of uneconomic collieries, assisting both re-deployment within the industry and re-settlement in others; it would write off about £400 million of the Board's £960 million capital debt to the Exchequer, giving about £30 million annual revenue relief in interest payments (which in 1964–5 had been a total of £42·7 million. Frederick Lee, then Minister of Power, had explained to Parliament that the industry was substantially over-capitalised and that the burden of debt must be reduced to correspond with the realities of the situation and the industry's prospects). In government establishments, coal was given a 5 per cent preference of price over oil and the government considered that the electricity industry 'should' continue to give preferential treatment to coal. Direct subsidy for coal was not favoured; it 'would be inconsistent with the concept of a self-supporting industry'.

Pre-election discussion of the size of the coal industry by Labour spokesmen had tended to be based on provisional figures of 200 million tons per year as the stabilised size of the industry. But the White Paper saw coal improving its position by further concentrating production on the economic pits and expecting a market of 170–180 million tons by 1970. While it rejected the concept of an arbitrary rundown in production, the policy on coal saw the size of the industry as depending significantly on its success in reducing costs.

'Relieved of the double burden of unprofitable collieries and past capital debt, and with the successful prosecution of the National Coal Board's own policies for improving the health of the industry, the economic part of the industry should be able with rising productivity to increase its output and its market', concluded the section on coal. While this represented some degree of support in facing then-current market forces, it fell a long way short of the kind of policy needed to sustain a target of coal supplying 200 million tons a year of Britain's energy requirements, which had been reiterated in Parliament only a few months earlier by Frederick Lee, as an objective 'for the present'. (This stage of the battle for maintaining the industry had in fact already been lost when George Brown's National Plan was published between the dates of Lee's statement and the White Paper, for the plan quoted the lower range of 170–180 million tons by 1970; it was immediately rejected by Robens in a public statement.) There were also, of course, discussions of the position of oil, nuclear power, gas and electricity, but it will be more profitable to examine these in discussing the further White Paper which burst into public view after a loudly contentious gestation some two years later.

Proposals for any kind of aid for coal inevitably sparked off accusations of 'feather-bedding the coal industry' by the advocates of free play of short-term market forces as the way towards salvation for Britain, as well as efficiency for the industry itself. Robens relates how, in the spring of 1965, he had been nettled, by a campaign along these lines, to cite the generous treatment of other industries

compared with the coal industry which, since nationalisation in 1947, had not cost the British taxpayer a penny, although it had been quite substantially subsidised before nationalisation. The biggest beneficiary, of course, had been agriculture, which had received about £2,700 million in subsidies and grants over a ten-year period. The White Fish industry was being helped to the tune of £4½m. in a year and the Forestry Commission was handing over £2m. in that year to private growers and developers. The

Government had written off £110m. of the accumulated deficit of BOAC. British Railways had enjoyed the writing-off of part of their accumulated deficit to the tune of £475m. . . .

The justification for this writing-off of capital in the coal industry was of course that in respect of assets taken over the earning capacity did not correspond to the interest that had to be paid on the compensation stock (though this point seemed to me to receive scant mention), and the new capital had been invested to meet an expected demand for coal that was not materialising. The NCB's own figures were for an output of 240 million tons when the policy decision was made back in 1950; the Federation of British Industry at the time had urged planning for an output of 270 million tons.

BATTLES OVER POLICY

By the end of the financial year 1966–7 (the years had been changed to run to the end of March from 1962–3) the overall position reached can be seen at a glance from the set of charts in Fig. 6. The sales drive had proved unable to hold up the demand, and deep-mined output had retreated to about 170 million tons; manpower continued to fall while productivity reached a new record. Powerloading had been further extended and correspondingly a National Power-loading Agreement was introduced covering about 100,000 faceworkers, since managers and men recognised that traditional piecework systems for earnings had 'become inappropriate' (apart from other complications of producing local disputes). Further collieries were closed down and the Board made an operating profit which slightly exceeded its £28 million interest obligation.

This was also, sadly, the year when the Aberfan disaster shocked the nation. Many thousands of tons of tipped waste, made muddy by hidden streams, slid down a hillside engulfing a school, killing over 100 people, most of them young children. The tribunal set up to investigate the causes criticised the total absence of tipping policy but acknowledged that there was no guidance available either in legislation or from HM Inspectorate of Mines and Quarries. Naturally, the NCB immediately organised special inspections of all other colliery tips under its control and made alterations where they were necessary. Robens offered his resignation in a letter, stating 'my mind has never been free from the tragedy of Aberfan since that harrowing day', as the tribunal had found that the disaster could and should have been prevented and he felt bound by a tradition allied to that of the doctrine of ministerial responsibility. The minister, Richard Marsh, did not accept the offer and asked him to continue. Meanwhile the Board accepted, and immediately started to operate, the findings of the tribunal. Within the mines death and accident rates were further reduced but the Board felt that casualties were still too high; it introduced a new safety organisation and started a fresh campaign concentrating on collieries with particularly bad accident records.

On the positive side, the NCB began to produce coal under revolutionary conditions at Bevercotes colliery, the first pit in the world to be planned for a complete and integrated system of remote and automatic control. Alongside the remarkable technical developments were equally revolutionary agreements with the mineworkers for coal to be produced on eighteen shifts spread over a seven-day week. The agreement offered a new status to the miners, with new grades and improved holiday and sickness benefit. Since it was a productivity agreement, it was permitted by the government although it was made during one of our many periods of restrictions on raising incomes. The trial, in fact, proved to be ahead of its time in terms of the reliability of equipment, but it was a bold attempt to make a very big jump in mining techniques. Though it failed, the lessons learnt were applied by Board scientists and engineers in later developments.

On the negative side the Board had to acknowledge that a further strong competitor had entered the field – a bonus for the nation, but adding to the difficulties of the coal industry. The discovery of large deposits of North Sea gas meant the further erosion of a market for coal that had in any case been declining as the gas industry had been using ever smaller

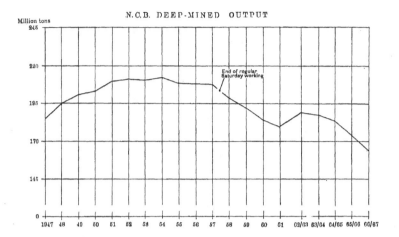

N.C.B. DEEP-MINED OUTPUT

Million tons

End of regular
Saturday working

1947 48 49 50 51 52 53 54 55 56 57 58 59 60 61 62/63 63/64 64/65 65/66 66/67

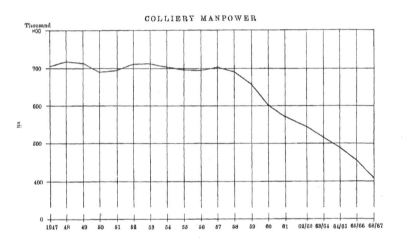

COLLIERY MANPOWER

Thousand

1947 48 49 50 51 52 53 54 55 56 57 58 59 60 61 62/63 63/64 64/65 65/66 66/67

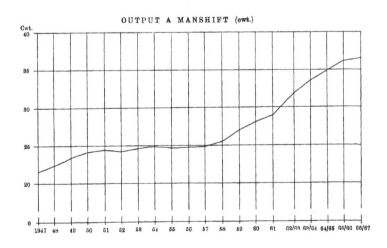

OUTPUT A MANSHIFT (cwt.)

Cwt.

1947 48 49 50 51 52 53 54 55 56 57 58 59 60 61 62/63 63/64 64/65 65/66 66/67

MECHANISED OUTPUT PERCENTAGE

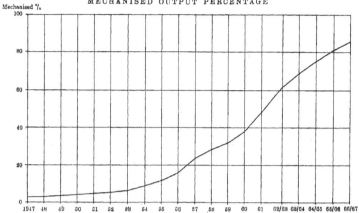

NUMBER OF N.C.B. COLLIERIES

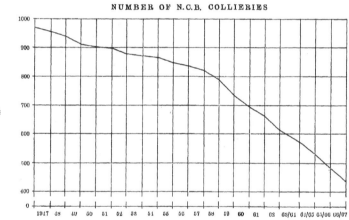

AVERAGE PROCEEDS PER TON

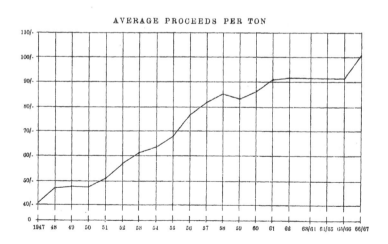

viii

quantities of coal gas, increasing its purchases of petroleum gases and making gas from oil fractions; furthermore, what had been a secondary fuel industry – at one time wholly dependent on supplies of premium coals – was now on the brink of becoming itself a primary source and taking part of coal's markets.

Great plans were also afoot for developing nuclear power – though in the event there were delays so that the share of total energy consumption supplied by nuclear electricity rose to 3 per cent by 1967 and has remained close to that level for a further seven years, despite enormous capital investment. The government accepted that the cost of providing electricity from nuclear stations would be less than that of generating in coal-fired ones but the Board, with Robens as their spearpoint, and Leslie Grainger – a Board member and an atomic energy expert – as their source of guidance on vital and sensitive points, vigorously and consistently disputed this, as I indicate in more detail below.

But how was the NUM reacting to this forced reduction of available employment for its members? Following a temporary surge of hope after the Labour government had been returned in 1964 when it was able to extract the qualified undertakings in the Commons from Frederick Lee (mentioned above) for assisting the industry's efforts to maintain a coal market of about 200 million tons, it was reduced to what amounted to a fighting retreat extracting the best terms it could for its members. During the whole period of contraction, it never had an industrial dispute on that issue (though there were many on others). The NUM's 1967 Annual Conference passed a resolution demanding that the government should underwrite the industry during 'an adequate transitional period in which to realise its full potential' and should assume the total social costs of reorganisation, but the NUM soon learnt that 'government thinking was running contrary to that of the union on this question'. It ran a series of meetings with the Prime Minister, the Minister of Power and other ministers, arranged a national demonstration, set out to influence public opinion and examined whether any kind of industrial action should be adopted since the government clearly was not going to take any measures to stabilise the market for coal. Rightly, it concluded

> . . . industrial action would do no good for the industry or the men employed in it; in fact it would be likely to reduce the coal burned and the result would be that the men employed in the industry would lose far more than they could possibly gain . . . the Union must continue with its efforts to influence public opinion . . . to maintain a viable industry of a size considerably larger than that at present envisaged . . . we rejected a proposal that there should be some kind of industrial action.

In the Commons, meetings were held of the Miners' Parliamentary Group and other MPs, questions were asked and pressure applied to the government which during 1967 was preparing a fresh statement of policy based on assuming fundamental changes in the pattern of energy supply following the dazzling promise of both the gas from below the North Sea and the unleashing of abundant cheap energy by transmuting matter in nuclear reactors. Robens very actively joined in the policy arguments.

How these struggles developed is recounted in very personal terms by Robens in his book, notably in chapters characteristically entitled 'Mixing it with Ministers' and 'Nuclear Scandals'. Saying that the nuclear programme was originally justified on the grounds that we had to take part in a new technological development and that it would generate electricity more cheaply than fossil fuel, Robens describes the cost prospectus quite simply as 'false'. He claims both that the capital cost of nuclear stations is higher (which everyone acknowledges) and that the electricity is dearer (which is the subject of dispute), apart from the issue of social costs that fell upon the nation since pits were closed down faster because their coal for making electricity was thus displaced. In addition, he recalls that the possible shortage of coal had been a factor in setting up the programme in 1955, but in 1957, when coal was coming into surplus, the government – far from curtailing the programme – set out to accelerate and speed up the construction of nuclear stations. This seemed unjustified for its time, and the result, quoted by Robens from a statement by Lord Penney in 1967 when he was Chairman of the Atomic Energy Authority, was that 'The country's first nuclear power station programme has not been as successful as expected – partly due to the fact that coal-fired power stations proved more economic, and capital and running costs for nuclear power stations higher, than expected'.

Despite statements by Sir Stanley Brown (Chairman of the CEGB) that there would be regular cuts in nuclear costings, Robens claimed in speeches that their costs were higher than coal-fired stations, that their capital costs were not being correctly charged, and that there was a hidden subsidy in not charging the very expensive research and development costs (or charging only a small token amount) so that in essence costs were being rigged to justify the nuclear energy programme. And, as a further blow, Robens added that about 10 per cent of the capital cost of that programme was in foreign exchange adding to the burden of the balance of payments, although in many discussions there had been an implication that it would relieve imports of fuel.

This case was made more formally in a memorandum by the NCB to the Select Committee on Science and Technology when it investigated the UK nuclear reactor programme in 1967. It disputed that Dungeness B would generate electricity more cheaply than other stations and more generally claimed that the AGR* could not be expected to have any economic advantage in the early 1970s. The greater initial capital investment would deny to the nation 'other industrial and social capital opportunities'. But the Ministry of Power in its reply stood by its calculations that nuclear costs would be reduced and defended the 'ground rules' used to calculate generating costs from nuclear and conventional power stations. (These turn on the method of operating power stations to cope with the wide variation in demand at different

*The Advanced Gas-cooled Reactors. The second generation of nuclear reactors using slightly enriched uranium dioxide fuel.

seasons and different times of day and are best examined in the original papers by the CEGB, the NCB and the Ministry).

Public debate was intensified when the CEGB announced that it intended to apply to build a nuclear power station at Seaton Carew on the Durham coalfield. Both the miners themselves, at the traditional Durham Miners' Gala, and the NCB pressed the government to make this a coal-fired station. When a figure was quoted for the cost of generation, Robens offered coal delivered to the station for $3\frac{1}{4}d.$ a therm, which would be competitive. This debate continued in many venues while the government considered its decision.

In general, at this period, the government was pressing the NCB for pit closures, but an exception was the occasion when the Prime Minister, Harold Wilson, speaking to the NUM on the eve of the Labour Party conference in 1967, announced that he had asked the NCB to postpone a number of closures from 1 October to 31 December. His request, said Mr Wilson, had been made

> in the light of an assessment of employment prospects during the coming winter. The case of each of the collieries concerned will be discussed with the chairman of the relevant regional planning council. . . . This does not represent a change in the government's long-term fuel policy, and after this winter the planned closure of uneconomic pits will continue as scheduled. However, to assist the industry during the period of transition, coal consumption at gas and electricity works will be boosted by 6m. tons a year and additional pensions will be available to men forced to leave the industry after the age of 55.

Earlier in the year, Richard Marsh (Minister of Power) had held a Fuel Policy Conference 'to establish the cheapest possible pattern of future energy supplies, compatible with the economic, social and technical realities of the situation', inviting the chairmen and senior representatives of the fuel industries. This study conference – again according to Roben's account – was the scene of furious battles, particularly over the comparative costs of coal-fired and nuclear-fired stations, and the intended future offtake of coal, or in practice the rate at which the industry would be run down. A high rate, pointed out Robens, would mean great difficulties within the coal industry in balancing wastage and recruitment, great problems in ensuring that men were absorbed elsewhere, and a rise in overhead cost of coal per ton since more of their capital assets would become unproductive and more capital would have to be written off. He quotes the first study documents as showing coal due to fall to 120 million tons in 1975 and only 80 million tons by 1980.

Though echoes of this 'confidential' gathering bounced around the press, they were as nothing to the reverberations of a later meeting – implicitly confidential – convened by Robens, of chairmen of Regional Economic Planning Councils (and the President and Secretary of the NUM) just five days before the 1967 White Paper was due to be published. Here, apparently continuing a policy of maintaining contact to try and dovetail pit closures with the advent of new industry to minimise unemployment, Robens outlined 'the dire prospects for each Region' of the planned rundown, by taking the forecast figures for coal consumption and converting them into probable manpower needed, taking account of expected rises in productivity. A mining force of 380,000 men in 1967 was due to decline to 159,000 by 1975 and to 65,000 by 1980; the NCB officers had worked out the implications of these national figures, region by region. When the meeting broke up and the press almost immediately got hold of this grim information, the effect was as electric as Robens must have foreseen. From his own report, the whole event seems technically to have been improper; the proceedings of the Fuel Policy Conference were private, the White Paper (for which it had been part of the preparations) was not yet published and, even if the invited chairmen had been asked to maintain confidence – which is not explicit in Robens's book – the material was so overwhelming and shocking that he must have expected it to leak. Presumably this was thought justified in view of the great human issues involved. Marsh almost immediately asserted that the figures were distorted. Robens writes of a following sequence of being attacked by ministers, praised by NUM lodges, pressed to resign by an MP in what he describes as an atmosphere of 'public brawling'. What, then, was in this policy document that was thus heralded by so many advance alarums?

FUEL POLICY 1967

'A review was needed', states the introduction to the 1967 White Paper *Fuel Policy,* 'not to re-examine the policy objectives set out in the White Paper of October 1965 which still stand, but to re-assess the balance between the available primary fuels (coal, oil, nuclear power and natural gas) and to set the framework for the most beneficial development of our energy supplies.' And the theme was that we were moving from a two-fuel economy – of coal and oil – to a four-fuel one, where nuclear power and natural gas would become major contributors. The government therefore aimed to see that our growing energy requirements were supplied in the way which yielded the greatest benefit to the country.

For the coal industry, the keynote can be summarised by the statement that, with certain safeguards, 'the Government's basic objective can be summarised as cheap energy', with the policy consequences that flowed from it. (Only seven years later the same department was advising exactly the opposite policy, of high-priced energy; one of its principal economists opened a newspaper article in 1974 by confessing 'I have shared in every major error in energy policy in this country over the last seven or eight years'.) With inescapable logic, it followed that:

Further decline in the markets for coal could not be prevented even by holding back the expansion of nuclear power and the development of natural gas unless the present level of coal protection were raised to an extent which would lead to a big increase in the general level of energy prices, or unless coal prices were heavily subsidised. But excessive protection for coal would lead to a misallocation of manpower and capital to the detriment of the economy as a whole.

This was switching the argument from the straight oil-versus-coal issue. The two newer fuels were seen as slowing down the advance of oil and taking up some of the markets coal would otherwise lose to oil. In effect, coal was already being seen as the residuary fuel, supplying whatever markets were left over from the other fuels. Nevertheless on social grounds some protection would continue to be given to coal, sustaining demand at 155 million tons in 1970. On this basis, the pattern of inland demand for energy was estimated at the levels shown in Table 12.

Table 12   *Primary fuel use*

	1966 (actual)	1970 (estimated)
	Million tons coal equivalent	
Coal	174·7	152*
Oil	111·7	125
Nuclear and Hydro-Electricity	10·2	16
Natural Gas	1·1	17
Total inland demand	297·7	310

*Plus an estimated 3 million tons for exports, making a total demand of 155 million tons.

Behind the very detailed statistical studies were a number of assumptions :

1 all gas available would be sold, taking two assumed quantities – high and low;
2 the second nuclear programme of 8,000 megawatts of capacity would be ready between 1970 and 1975, and a third large programme initiated;
3 the coal industry would achieve the expected increase in productivity;
4 no coal would be imported;
5 oil would continue to be available at a price competitive with coal;
6 gross domestic product would grow at a rate of about 3 per cent a year;
7 three possible courses on protection for indigenous fuels

would be examined – protection removed, current protection maintained, protection doubled.

The Six-Day War in the Middle East in June 1967, oddly, reinforced the sense of confidence in the safety of oil supplies (as Richard Marsh confirmed to me later). This apparently dangerous conflagration had had a negligible effect on supplies. So the White Paper quoted official thinking that it was

> right to base fuel policy on the expectation that regular supplies will continue to be available . . . difficult to predict the course of oil prices. There are a number of reasons for expecting them not to increase . . . it seems likely that oil will remain competitive with coal, and that pressure to force up crude oil prices will be held in check by the danger of loss of markets.

From this stemmed a policy for the coal industry of running down manpower at a rate of 35,000 a year, further financial support to the electricity and gas industries to use more coal during a transition period, aid to coal-mining areas, increased provision for financing deficits by the Board, and raising the Board's borrowing limit.

The scheme for financial support for the electricity industry to enable it to burn more coal than it would have done on purely economic grounds was stated to extend to 1970, and the gas industry was warned off from supplying fuel for generating electricity. For future power stations, the generating boards were told to 'base their choice of fuel on an economic assessment of the method of generation which will enable them to supply electricity at the lowest system cost consistent with security of supply and load balancing'. The government had been impressed with the massive increase in ordering of nuclear power stations in the USA and had therefore re-examined the economics of the second nuclear power programme and of longer-term nuclear costs against coal-firing. There are complications in these comparisons which are fully aired in an appendix to the White Paper, because coal was being supplied at a range of prices and because nuclear power stations are intended to be operated in a different way from coal-fired (being used at high load factors). But some of Robens's accusations on favourable systems of charging seem to be borne out. This, for example, is part of the discussion on the prices paid to the Atomic Energy Authority (AEA) for nuclear fuel, by the generating boards.

> Although the full costs arising from the provision of uranium and the re-processing of radioactive waste are not at present covered in the Trading Fund [for AEA activities of a commercial nature] as such, they are expected to be by the early 1970s, and by then the Atomic Energy Authority will be recovering all avoidable costs. As regards the Atomic Energy Authority's research and development expenditure, the royalty at the rate of 0·014d. per kWh. to be paid by the generating boards to the Atomic Energy Authority on AGRs in the second nuclear power programme has rested primarily on the assumption that they will show a cost advantage over alternative methods of generation. The royalty will not recover all the past costs of the development of the Magnox and AGR systems, but it is expected to cover all forward avoidable costs likely to be incurred by the Atomic Energy Authority in further development work for the second nuclear power programme.

As Robens observes, the NCB had paid for the whole of its research effort.

The same day a Coal Industry Bill was published to implement the proposals of the White Paper, and Anthony Crosland, President of the Board of Trade, announced the measures of aid for areas affected by colliery closures. For example, major industrial estates were to be established at Cramlington (Northumberland), Meadowfield (Brandon, Co. Durham), Bridgend (Glamorgan), and in Scotland and Wales. Extra incentives to new industry would be made available in areas of exceptionally high unemployment. But the critically important White Paper – presumably because of the intense opposition it aroused among the government's own supporters – was never debated in Parliament.

SUGGESTED FURTHER READING

Lord Robens, *Ten Year Stint* (Cassell, 1972)

National Coal Board, *Annual Reports and Statements of Account* for the individual years 1962 to 1967 inclusive

Second Report from the Select Committee on Nationalised Industries Gas, Electricity and Coal Industries (HMSO, 1966)

Fuel Policy, Cmnd 2798 (HMSO, 1965)

Fuel Policy, Cmnd 3438 (HMSO, 1967)

Meeting Europe's Energy Requirements. Memorandum by the West European Coal Producers and the National Coal Board (1963)

An Energy Policy for Western Europe. West European Coal Producers and the National Coal Board (1966)

E. F. Schumacher, 'Die europäische Kohle im Jahre 2000', *Politische Welt,* 51 (November 1962)

E. F. Schumacher, *Morgen noch Öl?* (1963) (text of lectures given in Germany)

E. F. Schumacher, 'Nuclear Energy and the world's fuel and power requirements', Paper for FBI conference on nuclear energy (1958)

Select Committee on Nationalised Industries. Sub-Committee A, Ministerial Control of the Nationalised Industries. Minutes of Evidence (HMSO, 1967)

Annual Reports of Conference of the National Union of Mineworkers, particularly the National Executive Committee Reports for the years 1964 to 1967 inclusive

Energy for the Future. Report from the working party authorised by the Council of the Institute of Fuel (Institute of Fuel, 1972)

20 Year Review of the Coal Industry, 1947–1966/67. Statistics Department, National Coal Board

Report of the Select Committee on Science and Technology Session 1966–67. United Kingdom Nuclear Reactor Programme (HMSO, 1967)

CHAPTER 9

Coal yields further ground

Thou shalt not kill; but need'st not strive
Officiously to keep alive
> Arthur Hugh Clough, 'The Latest Decalogue'

Throughout the coal industry there was a sense of outrage when the White Paper finally appeared. Morale was severely affected; the industry and the miner's MPs had campaigned vigorously and had seemed to be winning the arguments, especially against nuclear power. But, as far as the government was concerned, its approach to the four-fuel economy was summarised in a popular version of the White Paper as bringing the advantages of

1 growing amounts of high grade, clean fuel from our own resources;
2 lower energy costs;
3 less risk of growing over-dependent on other countries;
4 a boost to technological advance.

The NUM – evidently feeling itself in a weak position in a rapidly declining market – pressed in obvious directions for more support for the coal industry, for cutting back the second nuclear power programme, for banning the import of fuel oil and for appraisals of the social costs of the policy. But government policy – again quoted from the popular pamphlet summary – was for swift progress towards cheaper energy, 'at a pace which the fuel industries and the nation can handle without social dislocation and economic waste'.

Inexorably the policy led on to the battle of Seaton Carew – or, more precisely, the battle over the fuel to be used in this new power station sited on the Durham coalfield. 1967–8 saw a continuation of the pattern of coal consumption noted earlier. The overall total had again fallen, exports were negligible, almost all classes of consumer were taking less, the striking exception being power stations where consumption was up almost 4 per cent on the previous year. At over 69 million tons, this single market was taking over 41 per cent of the total. Obviously if this were lost it would represent a particularly severe setback, striking at the one remaining area of expanding demand. According to Robens, there was a secret meeting after the 1967 Durham Miners' Gala involving Harold Wilson, the Prime Minister, James Callaghan, Chancellor of the Exchequer, Robens and the NUM national officers to press the government to make this a coal-fired station, and the miners were said to have left this meeting confident that the ministers had recognised the force of their case. And apart from many speeches in other public places, miners' MPs succeeded in arranging an adjournment debate in the Commons. But all in vain. In August 1968, Roy Mason, who had by then been appointed Minister of Power, announced government approval of the CEGB application to build a nuclear power station. The news was received with ever deeper consternation by the coal industry.

Robens, in his comments, adds two further points to those I have quoted earlier. They are that this was treachery to the miners, who were among the most loyal supporters of a Labour government, and that Roy Mason had been in office too short a time to be able to assess the issues. (As an ex-miner, of course, he compounded the offence against the miners by this decision, according to this line of argument.) To these serious charges, Roy Mason – the only former working miner who has become Minister of Power, or its equivalent – in a personal discussion, gave me the following answers.

In respect of the White Paper and its proposals for rapidly

running down the coal industry, the furious debates in public were mirrored within the government. After it was published, eleven junior ministers who were miners' MPs or involved in miners' constituencies met and expressed great concern to the government over the policy. But all the studies and forecasts appeared to justify it. On the choice of fuel for Seaton Carew, Mason discovered the decision when he was appointed and two days later called on the prime minister to see if it could be reversed. The prime minister told him that the issue had been the subject of prolonged studies and would have to be announced. The accusation that the government was so committed to nuclear energy that it rigged the costings or under-rated the hazards was completely wide of the mark. Many departments had been drawn into a long exercise on costs and all related aspects; the latter, Mason told me, included loss of employment in coal, loss of rail traffic, and effects on sensitive areas such as the Durham coalfield. The fact that the announcement had to be made when the House was in recess aggravated the bad reaction by the miners' interests. But Mason then set out to retrieve something for the interests of the miners by delaying the licence for starting work on further nuclear stations, though under pressure by the CEGB and the constructors, while he in turn urged on the CEGB that he wanted to see a coal-fired station in their programme. CEGB soon offered a 'package' for two nuclear, one oil-fired and one coal-fired station which was approved by the ministry while Mason was still minister, but not immediately announced. This was 'left on the desk' for announcement by Harold Lever who became the responsible minister, when the Ministry of Power disappeared as a separate entity, in a later government reorganisation.

This undisclosed history seems to refute a good deal of the content of the attacks on the Labour government and on individual ministers. Richard Marsh, in my discussions with him, put it even more strongly; it was politically suicidal for a Labour government to 'clobber' the miners, and only the strength of the case for running down uneconomic pits, concentrating the industry and making it more competitive forced it into this policy, without which it saw no future at all for coal.

The replies answer all points except a basic one. Why was the growing strength of OPEC not foreseen? The forward estimates of Dr Schumacher and the West European Coal Producers organisation drew attention to the fact that demand for oil was growing faster than future ability to supply, so that OPEC's bargaining position would strengthen and prices rise. And although this was self-interested pleading, so would be the case from each of the fuel industries, and it was the business of government to make the right assessments of the international trends in a market so greatly influenced by world supply/demand relationships. The White Paper did not include a section on assessing international trends. Reference to the problem was made in these terms :

A wider question sometimes posed is whether world oil reserves are adequate. There is certainly oil in the ground to meet the world demand well beyond the period under review, and the danger is rather one of being denied normal supplies by political or other events outside the control of the industry or the government. In the longer term this danger is limited by the fact that producing countries are at least as dependent on trade in oil as we are ourselves, . . . Supplies can . . . be reorganised with speed and efficiency in the event of an interruption.

It is not clear whether this issue formed part of the 'wide-ranging statistical exercises' for the White Papers based on advanced mathematical 'models'.

Two independent studies carried out about this time – by the Economist Intelligence Unit and by the Brookings Institute of America – separately came to the conclusion that the coal industry was being run down too quickly; but these had no impact on government policy.

SELECT COMMITTEE

A further detailed review of the performance of the NCB by the (naturally all-party) Select Committee on Nationalised Industries in 1969 – there had been a number of others earlier

– opened its report by considering the interesting question of the amount that the Exchequer would save if assistance to the coal industry and protection were withdrawn. It noted that considerable extra unemployment benefit would have to be paid, there would be extra benefits due and the measures taken to promote new employment might be very expensive. Though electricity would become cheaper, income from fuel oil duty would be lost, and more foreign exchange would be needed to pay for higher imports of oil and coal. Against any possible financial advantages – the report was doubtful if there were any and did not attempt to quantify – it saw serious effects on the coal industry and further erosion of the market for coal. On balance, it saw the prospect of withdrawing these forms of support as a remote possibility.

While it thought that the Board was over-playing the risk of loss of morale in the industry due to the rate of closures, the Committee congratulated the Board, the NUM and the other trade unions concerned on their record of co-operation in the difficult circumstances – establishing a high standard of industrial relations and lessening the problems of the industry in its period of heavy contraction. It was worried about employment in developing areas, when pits were closed down, and floated the idea of a limited scheme of a premium on marginal coal-mining in these areas, not to alter the total of coal sold, but to divert coal-mining from areas with a low rate of unemployment to those where miners do not find other employment when they became redundant. In the long term the Committee saw NCB production as needing to be equated to demand; uneconomic capacity should be eliminated wherever possible as the only way to produce low-cost coal and retain a market for coal. In turn this meant that the future of the coal industry must lie mainly with the low-cost collieries of the central coalfields.

For this review, the NCB made extraordinarily optimistic forecasts of productivity rises to the Select Committee – from 47 cwt per manshift in 1969–70 to 75 cwt in 1975–6 – leading to estimates of a demand of 135 million tons at that time, since costs would fall to 80s. 10d. per ton from 93s. 6d. in 1969–70 (based on generally constant prices in the national economy). The ministry made its own independent estimate amounting to 120 million tons for 1975 but emphasised that this was not a target; its forecast was an assessment of what was likely to happen on a variety of assumptions. The Committee discussed these differences in an inconclusive way but evidently felt sceptical about the NCB figures since it advised the Board to make estimates of the effect on its productivity of a forecast of demand at levels other than 135 million tons.

An interesting theme briefly examined by the Committee when it was looking at the costs and benefits of the programme of closing collieries is the distinction between resource cost and accounting cost. The latter dealt with financial aspects; the resource costs are the true costs to the community of any action taken measured by the value of the resources employed – manpower, capital, material and foreign exchange. (The Ministry's general approach had been outlined in a memorandum to the Nationalised Industries Committee of Session 1967–8.) It appeared to be this concept that led the Select Committee to make the tentative suggestions of a premium for retaining coal-mining in areas of high unemployment – though the idea does not seem to have been pursued. The Minister of Technology, in an official set of 'observations' on the Report, undertook to consider this recommendation, but the democratic process shortly swept him away.

DIVERSIFICATION – OR 'HIVING OFF'?

Although, in practice, the Conservative Party has carried through major nationalisation, such as the Rolls-Royce take-over, in principle it is the Labour Party that favours extending public enterprise while the Conservatives aim to set the scene for developing private ownership of companies. When the Conservatives won the 1970 general election, it was Sir John Eden – who had the reputation of being a hardliner on dismantling the nationalised industries – who was appointed as a Minister of State with responsibility for those industries. In respect of coal, he soon opened discussions with Robens on hiving off the ancillary activities that had developed around the direct coal-getting and selling; the new government steered through a Coal Industry Act giving the minister the right to issue directives in effect enabling him to demand that the industry shed these side-activities. How had these auxiliary enterprises developed?

As mentioned earlier, the old colliery companies had extended their interests well outside the productive assets directly essential for mining coal. Some were linked with iron and steel works, manufactured fuel plants, coke ovens and allied works, and brick and pipeworks (based on the clays and shales associated with coal). There was a large acreage of farmland, waterworks, wharves and many other apparently strange properties for coal-owners. When the mines were nationalised, many of the non-mining assets were sold. But Robens, the public entrepreneur, had received approval from the previous (Labour) government to engage in a range of activities allied to mining. His policy he summarised as being

> to utilise our own resources, physical and human, our own particular expertise, which a shrinking mining industry had made available. The aim was to produce profits which we could use to help stabilise the price of coal and thereby improve the financial position of our primary business.

When the distributors of domestic coal-burning grates prevented the NCB from selling through its own showrooms (by threatening sanctions against the appliance makers) the Board bought a majority share in a builders merchant business and extended its chain. The Board also became a partner in a successful group drilling for gas and one foraging for oil; in both cases it pointed out that it was contributing expertise in drilling and geological exploration off-shore, not simply engaging in a financial partnership. The NCB association with Dutch State Mines in the Nypro venture making caprolactam for nylon 6 became very widely known in an unhappy context in the summer of 1974 when a major explosion killed twenty-eight men, demolishing the plant. The background to this venture had been a linking up with the chemically widely-experienced Dutch organisation to up-grade the market for crude benzole produced in carbonisation plants.

Probably the strangest of these developments, though still a logical one, was the sale of the spare capacity of the computers originally installed for normal internal duties – payroll, stores, invoices and the like. The aspect that at one stage received some press attention was the establishment of International Reservations Ltd, a service for booking hotel rooms run in collaboration with an American firm, covering hotels in the UK, North America and Switzerland. This arose from Robens's membership of the National Economic Development Council, where he saw a report on the hotel industry which gave him the idea of using the spare capacity on NCB computers. Later he extended the service to include hiring cars too. More directly in the mainstream of its business, the NCB had taken over some retail fuel distribution arrangements and extended them, the largest being a network set up with Amalgamated Anthracite Holdings Ltd, which was then further expanded to cover more of the west of England.

Although International Reservations made losses, most of the diversification proved successful. For example, in the Annual Report for 1971–2 the Board recorded that ancillaries, excluding those associated with carbonising coal and treating by-products, were being treated as one of its four main operating activities. The ancillaries provided an important contribution to the Board's overall finances and made profits of £7 million in that year, an increase on the previous year. It was the threat to this enterprising network, wrote Robens, that finally persuaded him to leave, although he was invited to stay as Chairman for a third term of five years. Mr D. J. Ezra, the former Deputy Chairman, succeeded Lord Robens as Chairman in July 1971.

This threat to the non-mining enterprises died down in due course (in fact, as mentioned earlier, the Conservative government actually became a nationaliser and intervener helping sick industries). When a major set of these interests was sold in 1973, namely the brickworks that had made the NCB the second largest manufacturer in the country, the sale was attributed to ordinary commercial factors. The NCB announced that 'the individual logic for the Board's involvement in these activities had declined over the years with the reduction in the use of colliery shale in brickmaking and in the consumption of bricks in colliery operations'. And the Board made over £2 million profit on the book value.

OTHER DEVELOPMENTS

Early in 1971 the Association for Coal in Europe published a fresh reappraisal of the energy resources for Western Europe, pointing out that the world situation had totally changed from that of the previous decades when oil was abundant. The USA – the nation consuming the largest amount of energy in the world – had become an oil and gas importer, and was planning to produce gas and oil products from coal. Demand for energy continued to grow rapidly throughout the world, notably in Western Europe, the USSR and Japan. In absolute figures the demand had risen from 4,400 million tons coal equivalent (mtce) in 1960 to 6,600 mtce in 1969 and could reasonably be expected to attain 12,000 mtce by 1980.

The principal consuming regions of the world – except the USSR – showed energy deficits, and the only areas with large surpluses available for export were the oil-producing countries of the Middle East and Africa. Their position would become stronger and so would their negotiating power, while that of the buyers would become weaker.

> For some years the countries of Western Europe have been privileged customers for Middle East Oil. But in the future they will find themselves in growing competition with the USA, Japan, the developing countries and perhaps even the countries of the Soviet bloc for a share of the Middle East's oil surplus . . . the underlying tendency in the world energy market will in the future be towards hardening of prices.

The Association, comprising the coal industries of Great Britain, Germany, France, Spain, Belgium and the Netherlands, consequently again urged the importance of preserving a substantial basis of indigenous fuel supply, particularly of solid fuels. Logic compelled it also to include the desirability of developing the production of indigenous oil, natural gas and nuclear power. But basically, like ancient prophets crying out to the foolish West European authorities to repent, and turn from their sinful ways that were leading them surely to destruction, the Association called for a change in the direction of European energy supply policy. The trends in the world fuel market made it clear that Western Europe should retain its output capacity for coal and end the contraction, or might have real difficulty in maintaining adequate supplies.

From a more independent source came similar warnings and recommendations in 1972. The Institute of Fuel, over-coming its reluctance to become 'politically involved' by working on a fuel policy, decided that widespread concern about future resources of energy justified it in setting up a small working party to develop proposals. The very first of its conclusions was this:

> The availability of reasonably priced oil to meet the pro-jected increased demand over the next 20 years is in doubt. Part of this demand should be reallocated to indigenous fossil fuels (particularly coal) and nuclear fuel; leaving oil to supply those markets where no alternative fuel is possible.

The Institute saw coal as becoming more important in the fossil fuel market during the next two decades – a remarkable observation when the fuel had been pushed out of one market after another for fifteen years – but pointed to the importance of controlling prices, notably by encouraging automated mining methods. The policy advocated was presented as a group of seventeen recommendations, some with sub-sections, and covered such themes as depletion policy for North Sea oil (which by then was seen as a coming source), nuclear energy including work on fusion as well as fission systems, several fuel efficiency topics, and the establishment of an Energy Commission to co-ordinate all sides of energy research.

Although the future was seen as depending heavily on nuclear power – forecast as taking over a large part of the increase in energy demand by 1990 – the working party saw nuclear power as the biggest problem in projections. Technical problems had arisen with both the first generation of gas-cooled thermal reactors (the Magnox type) and the advanced gas-cooled reactors (AGR). Apparently disagreeing with the claims of the CEGB, the Institute stated that at that time 'the aim of electricity being produced from nuclear fuel more cheaply than from fossil plants has rarely, if ever, been achieved'. Further problems had been encountered with the High Temperature Gas Cooled Reactor (HTR). Though the problem of depleting uranium resources could be overcome by applying breeder reactors producing more fissionable material, this technology was by no means proved. So for the EEC, depending on imports for 64 per cent of its energy needs, and for the UK, immediate policy would be to halt the rundown of the coal industry. The Institute also, incidentally, with some prescience, urged a world-wide programme of energy conservation (and pollution control) with the UK taking the lead and making available technology for using fuel as efficiently as possible.

Immediately before Britain formally entered the EEC on 1 January 1973, the coal industry published a re-appraisal of energy policy for Western Europe reiterating that the days of cheap and abundant energy were coming to an end, and that security of supplies was becoming a major issue. Their report, entitled 'Coal and Energy Policy in Europe' and issued jointly by the NCB, the British Association of Colliery Management, National Association of Colliery Overmen, Deputies and Shotfirers, the NUM, and the Institution of Mining Engineers, gives the impression of being an exercise in internal good relations and mending fences (after the traumatic national strike discussed below) as much as a document to influence public opinion and government. Adding to the case for coal on general energy grounds, the report also made the case for retaining a Community coal industry to provide the major part of coking coal for the steel industries. This had been analysed in some detail in the ACE appraisal and the NCB one simply summarised the trend as indicating growing pressure on coking coal supplies throughout the world, with grave doubts attaching to further availability and price of American coking coals, which provided the greater part of the imports of coking coal in the EEC.

In Britain the government in December 1970 lifted the ban on solid fuel imports, reviewing the decision early in 1972, but deciding to continue imports on an open general licence. In 1971 about 4 million tons were imported by the CEGB and 600,000 tons by the British Steel Corporation; other smaller amounts made up the total to 5½ million tons. About half came from the USA, large contribution from Australia and smaller quantities from elsewhere. Coal was still being imported in the following two years at prices about double those of the smaller quantity of exports. These shortages of coal due to too rapid rundown led to c.i.f. costs for imported coal amounting to £39 million in 1971 and £49 million the following year (aggravated by the effects of the strike), but falling to £21 million in 1973. Yet, though the costs of coal continued to rise, there was also a significant movement in the prices to be paid for imported crude petroleum, including refinery feedstock. After falling from £7 per ton in 1963 to a little over £6 by 1966 the price had returned (after a short-term larger rise around the period of the Six-Day War in the Middle East) to £7 in 1970. But in the following year it rose almost £2 a ton, in a preliminary flexing of muscles by the oil exporters, before 'taking off' as described in the following chapter.

WHEN A PIT CLOSES

What actually happens when a pit closes? At various stages I have referred to the concern which was expressed over the social effects of the rundown. The repercussions naturally attracted the attention of a number of social investigators, often sponsored by what was then the Ministry of Labour. In the North-East, for example, Professor J. W. House and Miss E. M. Knight of the University of Newcastle upon Tyne made a detailed survey of the economic and social effects of closing and reorganising collieries around Houghton-le-Spring in County Durham. With the co-operation of local organisations and the NCB, they examined what happened to transferred miners, redundant miners, and the men who simply left mining, as well as carrying out community studies in two villages, one intensely affected by closures and the other completely untouched by them. Contrasting the 'painless transformation' in Britain due to the policies of the NCB with the more 'turbulent outcome in the Ruhr of West Germany, the Borinage of Belgium or the Central Massif coalfields of France', the researchers nevertheless found the community affected by the rundown to have been impoverished in a number of ways; financially, they were poorer because of premature retirements, socially, they found leisure life impaired because of both the financial strain and the decrease in leisure time due to a much longer journey to work. Seventy per cent were transferred to neighbouring pits immediately, redundancies amounted to 17 per cent and voluntary wastage was 9 per cent. (The shortfall is not accounted for.) And though the detailed analysis picks out effects and notes that the men over 55 had particular difficulties, the overall summary reasonably concludes :

> The effects of mining changes around Houghton have therefore not been dramatic and the character of the communities has largely been continued. Nevertheless among those directly affected the impact has been substantial.

A similarly detailed survey was made directly under the auspices of the ministry (again with the collaboration of the NCB, NUM and government departments) on the closing of Ryhope colliery, also in Co. Durham and not very far from Houghton. Durham, of course, had a particularly heavy closure programme, and the Board wished to apply a long-distance transfer scheme for men to go to the Central Coal-fields in Yorkshire and the Midlands. The House inquiry had been devoted to effects of past closures. The one covering Ryhope started in advance, covering the time from six months before the event to one year after. Since an earlier study had shown that many men had not been aware of the opportunities elsewhere and of the system of transfer allowances, a van was stationed at the colliery to publicise the Board's 'Pick-Your-Pit' Scheme. Both Board and researchers found in the men a deeply-rooted attachment to the locality and its associated network of relationships. Consequently, moving meant weighing up possible material gain against the loss of 'community sanctuary'. Nevertheless, overall, a large measure of success was found in the local and the long-distance redeployment. A major exception reported by the researchers was in dealing with the redundant men – a relatively small group, including a high proportion again of men over 55 – 'stranded by the tide of industrial change, technological advances and discoveries [who] confront the nation with a social, economic and moral problem'.

The findings in detail are of some complexity and cannot be dismissed simply with a glib phrase as being deeply worrying or wholly reassuring. They indicate the extensive disturbances caused by the closures within these tightly-knit special communities and how many families have been able to cope with them; but the results of this kind of advance-planned shutdown, with aid from both the publicly-owned industry and state agencies, are æons removed from the virtual murder of villages which occurred from time to time in the past in earlier closures of pits under private ownership and before state welfare activities were appreciably developed.

NATIONAL COAL STRIKE 1972

The silver jubilee of the nationalised coal industry was unfortunately marked by an official national strike in January/February 1972 lasting about seven weeks; it was the first since 1926 and followed a ten-week ban on overtime. The Board commented that until the start of the industrial action the industry had been achieving productivity levels indicating that its output and financial targets would be met. As a result of the action the prospective operating profit was transformed into an operating loss of £118 million. After a hearing by a Court of Inquiry and some further negotiations, the miners achieved most of what they had claimed. For surface workers, for example, the claim for craftsmen previously earning £18.35 a week had been for £26; the final agreement was for £23.35. In the case of face workers covered by the National Power Loading Agreement the earlier rate was £30, the claim £35 and the settlement £34.50. But between the claim and the settlement there had been a first response by the Board based on what is considered the commercial possibilities; these comprised assessing the effect on the market of a price increase to pay for the settlement and on the Board's financial commitments set out by successive governments. Knowing that the NUM Annual Conference had reduced the majority needed for approving a strike in a membership ballot to 55 per cent, the Board proceeded with further improved offers, but these were rejected. First an overtime ban was imposed by the NUM, then a strike ballot authorised the NUM executive to call for a strike. After the executive had duly given the Board a month's notice of the intention to strike, further efforts were made by the Board to avert this severe setback for the industry, but in vain. The strike itself was marked by a considerable amount of ill-feeling and the Board accused the miners of not carrying out safety duties agreed in guidance issued by the union itself and in preventing managers from carrying out safety duties in the pits. According to the NCB, the guidance was followed at only twenty-eight collieries out of 289.

The miners had conducted analyses of stock levels in various sectors of industry (the best equipped were the power stations with eight weeks' supply of coal) and received support from the TUC which had recommended members of affiliated unions not to cross picket lines. The NUM had sent pickets throughout the country to all major power stations, ports, coal depots, steel works, opencast sites and even reclamation tips, leading to considerable indignation by those affected though not feeling themselves directly involved in the primary dispute.

Early in February the government declared a state of emergency and soon there were large power cuts imposed on a rota basis throughout the country. From mid-February there were severe restrictions on using electricity, which was permitted on only three days a week. In Parliament, the Opposition (Labour and Liberal parties) moved to condemn the government for its failure to play an active part in seeking to bring about a settlement in the dispute, but the motion was lost. Mr Carr, Secretary of State for Employment, in various statements referred to the importance of lowering the level of pay settlements in order to reduce the rate of price increases, but had several sets of talks with both the NUM and the NCB.

The Court of Inquiry mentioned above comprised Lord Wilberforce (a Lord of Appeal in Ordinary) as Chairman, Mr John Garnett (director of the Industrial Society) and Professor L. Hunter (Professor of Economics, Glasgow University). After it had reported there were further alarums and negotiations involving a meeting between the two sides at 10 Downing Street before the strike was called off with an overwhelming vote of 96·5 per cent in favour of accepting the final settlement. In addition to the wage increases, the settlement included lowering the age at which the adult rates were to be paid at yearly intervals down to eighteen, five additional individual days of annual holiday, and taking the wage settlement as effective until the end of February 1973.

The background to this major national upheaval and the bitterness had been the declining position of miners in wages relative to other industrial workers. The NUM, in its report on the strike, referred to 'the solidarity and determination of the members born of the decline in their relative standard of living over the past five years'. The setback in coal within the national economy had been mirrored by a fall in the miners' position in the 'league table' of wages of industrial workers. In 1952 average weekly earnings in coal-mining had been about 28 per cent higher than the average for all manufacturing industries. By 1970 they were actually below. Even after the apparently large rises awarded they came up to only 5 per cent above, in a period of rising wage inflation. The Wilberforce Report – an extraordinarily interesting document, though compiled under great pressure in a few days – quoted the 'rank' of coal-miners out of twenty-one industry groups as having been third in October 1960, falling to twelfth by October 1970, with a small recovery in October 1971 due to the 1970 settlement in mining preceding a depression in earnings in manufacturing because of a recession in business conditions.

The Wilberforce Committee accepted that miners were truly a 'special case' – having working conditions among the toughest and least attractive of all – and that their pay levels should reflect this. Many of the surface workers, it said, are men who have had to be re-deployed from underground because their health has been adversely affected by working conditions, so that equity demanded that their pay levels should also be improved. Noteworthy among the miners' evidence was a memorandum by Michael Meacher, MP, on the 'poverty trap' that engulfs lower-paid workers in general, including some surface workers of the coal industry. A conjunction of factors including the incidence of income tax and the way means-tested benefits operate has the result that they do not gain anything from small increases in pay. Only relatively large ones enabled them to escape from the 'trap' and achieve any gain in net income. The Wilberforce Committee also recognised the limitations within which the Board had to work and again drew attention to the severe burdens of an unrealistic financial structure which limited what it was able to offer.

The strike was estimated to have cost 10·5 million working days of lost time in mining, and extensive lost time in other industries where almost 2 million workers were thought to have been thrown out of work for some part of the time. Though the output in the rest of the economy during the period of restricted power was considered remarkably high, it nevertheless obviously involved severe losses. For the Board, the strike left an immediate residue of three major problems, even though there was a virtually complete return to work and the gain in productivity was soon resumed. The problems were these :

1   A 'massive deterioration' in the financial position. To have corrected it fully by increasing prices would have meant a totally impracticable 25 per cent rise; to limit the effect on the market for coal (and minimise inflationary effects), the rise was in fact restricted to 7·5 per cent.
2   The fall in sales, where difficulties due to competition and some recession in industry had become aggravated by a loss

of reliability in supplies. Though the Board did not quote this in its Annual Report, the loss of confidence was very marked in the case of its largest customer, the electricity industry, which openly and loudly commented on this feature.

3 The restoration of industrial relations to encourage full and frank participation to achieve the best results for the industry. On this, the Board opened discussions with the NUM to try and 'agree with them a framework within which future negotiations over pay and conditions can take place so as to reduce the risk of a further confrontation which would have a perilous effect on the industry'. They started talks on a productivity element and on re-establishing an effective conciliation procedure to reduce the need to resort to industrial action. And the chairman of the National Reference Tribunal, which had been by-passed, sent letters to the NCB and the NUM reaffirming its impartiality and its willingness to serve the industry.

The Board's Chairman, Mr D. J. Ezra, made frequent conciliatory statements on the resilience of the coal industry, the speed of its recovery after the strike, the opportunities for the coal industry as the principal oil-producing countries in the Middle East and Africa showed their determination to obtain increasing oil revenues, and the need for coal to be operated with efficiency to provide a proper service to the public and for fair remuneration for the management and miners who work in it. The government made the necessary financial arrangements in support of the Board following the losses due to the strike. They included an Order increasing the permitted limit on the Board's accumulated deficit, an Order increasing the limit on the Board's borrowing power, and a Supplementary Estimate for an emergency grant of £100 million; other necessary measures were taken to ensure adequate supplies of coal for the country, notably the allowing of coal imports on general licence.

During the following year, the industry did indeed recover remarkably quickly from its wounds with o.m.s. rising to record levels, sales regained, stocks both distributed and NCB-held being rebuilt. But it also recovered something far more. For this appeared to be the year in which 'official' thinking began to turn and to recognise the dangers to the whole economy in increasing the nation's dependence on oil before nuclear energy and gas were beginning to make a major contribution.

The wind of change was evident in the speech of Tom Boardman, Minister for Industry, when moving the second reading of the Coal Industry Bill (cited in Chapter 1) which became the Coal Industry Act 1973 well before OPEC applied the larger turns of the screw. Future developments in the field of energy would mean that uncontrolled contraction of the coal industry would pose an unacceptable danger to the country's supplies of energy, said the minister. This was one of the compelling reasons for substantial government assistance, although the Board had to accept responsibility for ensuring that the industry operated viably within the new financial framework.

What were the main provisions? The Act

1   reduced the book value of the Board's assets and wrote off accumulated deficits, relieving the Board of about £40 million a year in depreciation and capital charges;
2   reduced the Board's borrowing powers from £950 million to £550 million which could be raised by Order to £700 million and set a ceiling of £50 million on accumulated deficit which could also be raised by Order;
3   permitted grants for 'social costs' for dealing with the re-deploying of men, redundancy payments, compensation for premature retirement, resettlement and removal costs;
4   provided a further sum of up to £60 million for 1973–6 or £100 million for 1973–8 for an improved and extended redundancy payments scheme;
5   provided grants to meet the cost of burning extra coal at electricity generating stations in preference to oil;
6   provided grants to finance part of the stocking costs for coal and coke and further grants for producers of coking coal supplied for use in the iron and steel industry, under the rules of the European Coal and Steel Community;

7   permitted regional grants to help the Board to 'moderate the contraction' of the industry in the development and other assisted areas, since there is a heavy concentration of mining in these areas;

8   increased the maximum permissible size of the Board by three part-time members so that the Board could comprise a Chairman and up to fourteen other members. The grants were maxima and the actual sums paid were due to depend on actual levels of expenditure, or were to be the subject of annual agreement with the minister.

The general mood at this time was one of confidence – improved consultation procedures, recovery of productivity and pressing forward with a series of measures to improve it further, setting up an Environmental Policy Group with duties including using up waste materials, an increase in the use of coal in the country – and even the beginnings of deliveries of natural gas from the Viking field to British Gas by the subsidiary National Coal Board (Explorations) Ltd. The economy was recovering, and on the industrial sales side the main aim was to restore confidence in coal's competitiveness and ability to supply.

Outside in the great wide world, major changes were under way which were due to have the most profound effect on the energy economy of the whole globe, and, because of the fundamental importance of energy to the industrialised countries, on the overall financial position of many nations, notably Britain. For the sheikhs and the Shah, the kings and presidents of the great oil-producing countries of the world, particularly the Arab countries, had begun to realise the stranglehold that they were in a position to exert on the rest of the world, and were tightening the squeeze which among other features very suddenly restored the importance of King Coal in Britain.

SUGGESTED FURTHER READING

National Coal Board, *Annual Reports and Statements of Account* for the individual years 1967/68 to 1973/74 inclusive

Digest of United Kingdom Energy Statistics 1974 (HMSO, 1975)

Energy for the Future. Report from the working party authorised by the Council of the Institute of Fuel (Institute of Fuel, 1972)

Lord Robens, *Ten Year Stint* (Cassell, 1972)

Fuel Policy, Cmnd 3438 (HMSO, 1967)

Report of the Select Committee on Nationalised Industries. Session 1968–69. National Coal Board. Vol. 1 *Report and Proceedings of the Committee.* Vol. 2 *Minutes of Evidence taken before sub-committee A and Appendices* (HMSO, 1969)

National Coal Board. Observations by the Minister of Technology Cmnd 4323 (HMSO, 1970)

Black Diamonds Silver Anniversary. 25 years 1947/72. National Coal Board

Fuel for the Future (HMSO, 1967)

Annual Reports of Conference of the National Union of Mineworkers for the years 1967 to 1973 inclusive

Energy Resources for Western Europe: Present Situation and Future Prospects (Association for Coal in Europe, 1971)

Coal and Energy Policy in Europe: A Report by the British Coal Industry (December 1972)

Coal Industry Act, 1973 (HMSO, 1973) and *Hansard*, 21 December 1972, for debate on Coal Industry Bill

Report of a Court of Inquiry into a dispute between the National Coal Board and the National Union of Mineworkers under the Chairmanship of the Rt Hon. Lord Wilberforce, CMG, OBE. Cmnd 4903 (HMSO, 1972)

John Hughes and Roy Moore (Eds), *A Special Case? Social Justice and the Miners* (Penguin Books, 1972)

J. W. House and E. M. Knight, *Pit Closure & The Community.* Report to the Ministry of Labour. *Papers on Migration and Mobility in Northern England No. 5.* (University of Newcastle upon Tyne, Department of Geography, 1967)

Ryhope: a pit closes. A study in redeployment (HMSO, 1970)

CHAPTER 10

The sheikhs take a hand

his words were softer than oil, yet were they drawn swords.

Psalms 55 : 21

During the course of 1973 oil was transmuted from a fuel that was cheap and abundant to one that was expensive and insecure. Behind this revolution were these historic trends.

In the first chapter I summarised the world energy pattern in recent years. As the events of the last few years have dramatically confirmed, the market for sources of energy is, above all, highly international in character. Since the Second World War, demand has grown at increasing annual rates; before 1973 the global growth rate was about $5\frac{1}{2}$ per cent a year, for Western Europe 6·3 per cent, and for Japan no less than 11·9 per cent. Coal had been losing ground to oil and gas. For Western Europe the annual rate of growth in using oil had been 10·5 per cent in the last decade, for Japan 17·5 per cent. The USA, in earlier years an oil exporter, had an average annual *growth rate in importing oil* between 1962 and 1972 of 8·4 per cent. Every one of these figures had been seriously under-estimated in forecasts by official agencies. In a review for a Royal Society conference in 1973 on the outlook for world energy, Joel Darmstadter reconsidered the earlier figures, set out a number of reasonable assumptions and bravely made a set of fresh forward 'guesstimates' of his own. From these he concluded that :

The net import requirements for oil of the United States, Western Europe and Japan combined are seen, in these assumptions, to rise from 23 million barrels/day in 1972 to around 52 million barrels/day in 1985, implying an average annual rise of 6·5 per cent and a cumulative thirteen-year total of about 183 billion barrels. [Here billion means 10^9.]

After relating these figures to the total proved reserves of the potential exporters – they are identical to those of Saudi Arabia – Darmstadter continues:

The indispensability of future Middle East supplies, and, apparently, of Saudi Arabia within the Middle East, in accommodating this particular demand-supply hypothesis stands out unmistakably.

New technologies such as coal gasification, coal liquefaction, the breeder reactor, solar energy, geothermal energy or fusion energy were not seen as likely to make a major contribution to commercial energy supplies before the 1990s at the earliest. Whether oil from shale could be produced at prices competitive with that from oilfields remained doubtful. Darmstadter therefore urged an internationally forward-looking policy to 'blunt the enormous economic advantage exercised by the major exporters over countries – both developed and less developed – . . . dependent on substantial amounts of imported energy for many years to come'.

But a new generation of Arabs, many of them trained in the business and scientific schools of the USA and Western Europe and at least equally able to read statistical tables and graphs, were quicker off the mark. In 1960 the Organisation of Petroleum Exporting Countries (OPEC) was formed by the governments of Iran, Iraq, Kuwait, Saudi Arabia and Venezuela. Later, other countries joined and in mid-1975 OPEC had twelve members – the others being Algeria, Ecuador, Indonesia, Libya, Nigeria, Qatar, and the United Arab Emirates (including Abu Dhabi). Gabon is an associate member. Its general aim, set out explicitly at its fourth conference in 1962, was to increase the share of oil revenue accruing to the producing countries. During the 1960s, it opened a series of negotiations to achieve this by a number of technical devices including an increase in the 'posted price' of petroleum on which tax is levied (even if this price is higher than that actually realised in the market). An important stage was reached at the 21st OPEC conference in 1970, after an earlier series of claims against the oil companies. From this, after various vicissitudes in various places, a new agreement was reached with the six Gulf states in February 1971 in Tehran giving further increases to the states with a system of fixed increases for the following five years and an undertaking by the countries concerned establishing 'security of supply and stability in financial arrangements for the five year period 1971–75'. This Tehran agreement was followed by agreements in the other oil-exporting countries. Its value was soon tested and found wanting.

By September of the same year OPEC had claimed compensation for the devaluation of the dollar leading to a fresh agreement in January 1972 on a further increase known as the Geneva Agreement. In one or other of the oil exporting countries, there were a series of demands for 'participation', or actual nationalisation or seizures during 1972 and 1973. By June 1973 there had been a further 12 per cent increase in posted prices forming the Second Geneva Agreement. Saudi Arabia, a little earlier, referring to the use of oil as a political weapon, had warned that it would not guarantee future increases in oil production if the US failed to support a political settlement in the Middle East acceptable to the Arabs. After the Second Geneva Agreement, OPEC indicated that the annual increases provided in the Tehran Agreement were not considered sufficient.

When Egypt and Syria attacked Israel in October of that year, among many other reactions of the oil-exporting states Kuwait called an Arab summit on the wider use of Arab oil as a political weapon. In rapid succession there followed immediate 70 per cent increases in posted prices by the Arabian Gulf producers, larger rises by Libya, a decision by the Organisation of Arab Petroleum Exporting Countries (set up in 1967 to represent their special interests in addition to the wider-based OPEC) to reduce supplies of oil progressively to countries unsympathetic to the Arab cause by 5 per cent each month, then a further decision for a total embargo on supplies to the Netherlands and the USA. On 1 January 1974 further rises came into effect, doubling the existing posted prices, though accompanied by what some called a Christmas bonus in a relaxation of the cut-back in production.

Different grades of oil have different prices. But the overall situation can conveniently be assessed in terms of the posted price of Saudi Arabian light crude, used as the 'yardstick' for the new price structure for the six Gulf states. On 1 June 1970 it was $1·80/barrel; after various intermediate steps the last turn of the screw at the end of 1973 sent it soaring to $11·651. Over this period the percentage increase amounts to 547. The Libyans did better by moving from $2·23 in June 1970 to $15·768, an increase of 607 per cent.

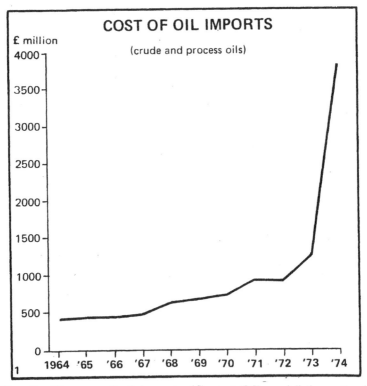

Fig. 7   The cost of oil imports. (Central Office of Information.)

The economic effect of transferring large blocks of revenue to the oil exporting countries, putting severe strains on the balance of payments of the consuming countries, has often been discussed. For Britain, the average landed cost of crude oil rose over this period from $14·47/metric tonne to $68 so that nationally the cost of oil imports rose in a way that can be more vividly appreciated from the simple graph shown in Fig. 7 than from tables of figures. And for some months while the Arabs continued to blow hot and cold over whether there would be cuts or not, there was grave anxiety over the continuation of supplies despite the strategic stocks that had been built up in the country and the whispers that the oil companies were obtaining and diverting supplies from other sources.

All this, it should be recalled, followed only a few years after senior officials at the Ministry of Power had advised that greater support for the coal industry was unjustified, that the coal industry should be quickly run down at a rate largely limited by social factors and, in the historic words of the 1967 White Paper, that it was 'right to base fuel policy on the expectation that the regular supplies of oil at competitive prices will continue to be available', thus concluding that 'no greater discrimination against oil should prove necessary on grounds of security'.

NATIONAL COAL STRIKE 1974

When the 1970 Conservative government came into office it disbanded the National Board for Prices and Incomes set up by its predecessor and declared its intention of curbing inflation by measures designed to 'squeeze' the economy and allow the working of the free market to control the movement of prices and incomes. By the end of 1972 the government had abandoned this policy and introduced a Statutory Prices and Pay Standstill; early in the following year it published policy proposals for a follow-up to this standstill, leading to a Price and Pay Code, to be regulated by two new agencies – a Price Commission and a Pay Board. Stage Two allowed certain increases in both prices and pay in strictly defined ways –

details are not relevant here – and was followed by Stage Three of this counter-inflation policy in October 1973. Wage increases were limited by statute to an average of either £2·25 a week, or if preferred 7 per cent with a limit of £350 a year, on the amount to be received by any one individual. Exceptions were allowed for certain specific situations such as changes in pay structures, better use of manpower, efficiency schemes, 'unsocial hours' and progress towards equal pay for women. Threshold agreements were included permitting pay increases of up to 40p a week for certain movements of the Index of Retail Prices until the end of Stage Three in November 1974.

Though many settlements were finalised under these conditions, the NUM when it made its claims during 1973 refused to settle within these limitations, again claiming that miners' relative pay had fallen; this further round of industrial struggle then developed against the backcloth of the oil supply situation described above – the miners clearly recognising their greatly enhanced bargaining power resulting from the oil crisis. The settlement was again close to the claim, the Pay Board acknowledging that 'the settlement following the Wilberforce inquiry in 1972 was a temporary gain which has since been eroded'.

But between the claim and the settlement there had been further turmoil and, in effect, the miners had toppled the Conservative government in a general election where settlement with the miners was a central issue. The Labour Party came before the electorate pledged to provide the conditions for an early fair settlement, and more or less by a hair's-breadth was empowered to act upon it. Finally, the main terms of the settlement between the Board and the NUM were these :

Pounds per week	1973	Claim	Settlement
Minimum surface	25·3	35	32
Minimum underground	27·3	40	36
Coalface (national power loading agreement)	36·8	45	45

There were also improvements in night allowance and holiday pay and a payment of £30 in place of a third week's holiday, and some others. Before this outcome, there had been an overtime ban by the miners in November 1973 which developed into a full national strike a couple of months later. Meanwhile the government had declared a state of emergency, then ordered that industry work only a three-day week; there were also severe limitations on heating and lighting in order to conserve coal and electricity. In support of the miners and their claim that they were a 'special case', the TUC issued a declaration that its member unions would not invoke any settlement with the miners outside the Stage Three legislation in support of their own claims; but the government decided that it would nevertheless not waive its legislation.

The Board had earlier used all possible loopholes within the rules, for example, on payments for unsocial hours, to offer what was in effect a 17 per cent increase. The government referred the claim to the Pay Board to determine whether there was a special case justifying exceptional treatment. In an atmosphere of growing confrontation between the government and the miners, Mr Heath, the Prime Minister, dissolved Parliament and called a general election in which he saw the main issue as the attempt by the NUM to use its industrial strength to defeat the policy of an elected government. The Labour Party severely criticised the whole approach of confrontation, widening its campaign to include the full range of the government's policies and its general record. After the February 1974 election, the final strengths of the parties were:

Labour	301	Liberal	14
Conservative	296	Others	24

There was some political skirmishing while Mr Heath attempted to form a coalition, but failed. Labour formed a government and Mr Wilson appointed Mr Michael Foot, as Secretary of State for Employment, to proceed immediately to settle the dispute.

A little earlier the Pay Board had produced a report on the problems of pay relativities, setting out the general principles that lay behind the determination of pay. But it was asked to go beyond principles, as mentioned above, and make specific recommendations on the miners. Its report, published shortly after the election, confirmed that average weekly earnings of male manual workers in mining had indeed fallen back from a ratio of 105·6 per cent of those in manufacturing industries in 1972 to 102·3 per cent the following year. In essence the report pointed out that the long-run contraction of the industry would have to be reversed in the new circumstances and that higher relative pay would be necessary to recruit and retain sufficient mineworkers. The incoming Labour government immediately accepted the case and the recommendations.

OPEC manoeuvres, as well as the trends in other manual workers' wages, had played a large part in the thinking of the Pay Board, in recommending 'exceptional' payments to mineworkers which would mean an increase in the NCB's wage bill of £95 million instead of about £44 million as offered. Recent sharp increases in oil prices, the Pay Board noted, meant that the NCB was now directing its efforts to increase capacity instead of continuing the reduction. Merely to halt the long period of decline, it appreciated, represented a major change of policy and would impose many problems of investment, production and manpower. Even allowing for the statistical difficulties and differences (there had been public debates on whether certain comparisons were valid, e.g. between figures for wages that took into account holiday payments or other allowances and others that did not), the Pay Board concluded that 'there can be no doubt that the relative position of coal mining *vis-à-vis* manufacturing has changed considerably over the years'. The Pay Board acknowledged the unique situation regarding health hazards and the special unpleasantness and disadvantages of coal-mining. On cost comparisons, it noted the large rises in the price of oil and the result that the current cost of fuel oil for power stations was between 6p and 7p a therm (including 0·6p excise duty) so that 'coal could now compete with fuel oil with some limited room for manoeuvre'. For the true cost of coal, excluding all state subsidies but including the NCB offer costing £44 million, was less than 5p per therm. The extra £50 million would cost about 0·2p per therm – according to a further calculation by the Pay Board.

The detailed arrangements finally agreed by the NCB and NUM were somewhat different from those proposed by the Report, but since OPEC had made coal competitive and the government had approved the general approach of the Pay Board, the global sum agreed remained close to that of the recommendation.

ARRESTING COAL'S DECLINE – PLANNING FOR GROWTH

An extra £2,000 million annually to be added to our import bill – this was the government estimate of the likely effect on the UK of the new oil prices – adding to an already serious deficit in the balance of payments. And, while the dazzling vision for the middle future was the income-to-come from North Sea oil, there remained the problem of the intervening years before the early 1980s when both the Treasury and the oil companies expected that Britain would be meeting all its energy needs from indigenous sources. From being one of the lesser considerations of government and most of industry (obviously apart from the big fuel users – electricity, iron and steel, cement, glass, pottery), energy supplies were transformed into a major issue affecting the very financial stability of the whole kingdom. There was grave concern about financing the expected major debts to the oil-supplying countries, a problem that was eased when they decided to place large deposits in the City of London. Nevertheless the repercussions hit the whole of the country – in common with the rest of the world – and leaders warned that this enormous transfer of purchasing power must involve some lowering of the standard of living. When the Chancellor of the Exchequer, Mr Healey, announced measures intended to slow down the rate of inflation in July 1974, he gave as the main reason for the rate of retail price increases the unprecedented rise in the price of commodities – above all, oil. Consequently, as a Department of Energy memorandum put it :

The massive change in energy prices since the autumn of 1973 has brought about a situation in which the replacement of imported, and expensive, energy by economically produced home substitutes must be the main thrust of energy policy. It has also moved energy conservation into a much higher place in the scale of policy values . . .

Overall, consequent government policy included a third nuclear power station programme, and a review of continental shelf policy, refinery policy and proposals to control the rate of depletion of deposits under the North Sea; but a major part was a re-examination of attitudes to the coal industry.

Though a Treasury review of the changing energy situation at this time, wrote, almost with an air of surprise, of the world oil crisis as having 'abruptly ended the period of cheap and abundant oil supplies enjoyed since the 1950s', the Board – evidently believing its own forecasts – had been engaged from early 1973 in preparing production plans for new capacity 'with the aim of enabling the industry to take advantage of the new opportunities created by the developments in the energy market and by an anticipated improvement in coal's competitive position in relation to oil'. Yet, even the Board found that 'the oil price revolution came sooner and more dramatically than expected'.

Its studies culminated in a *Plan for Coal* based on an expansionist investment programme with a capital cost of £600 million to develop new deep-mined and opencast capacity and greatly expand research on mining and applications of coal. Soon after the new Secretary of State for Energy, Mr Eric Varley, had taken over, a so-called 'tripartite examination' of the future of the industry was initiated, the three parties being the government, the NCB and the unions. Introducing the resulting final report, Varley emphasised that reversing the decline of the previous fifteen years was a formidable task, implying that this was under-estimated by those outside the industry. Further government backing was promised with 'faith' in the industry and a 'commitment to its present and future success'. Specifically, support was due to take these forms:

1   a contribution of around £100 million towards an NCB scheme to provide early compensation of up to £10,000 to pneumoconiosis sufferers – their health damaged by much earlier negligence in controlling dust;
2   financial help in relieving existing deficiencies in pension funds to assist in establishing an improved and earnings-related scheme for mineworkers;
3   endorsement of an expanded programme of long-term research and of developing new uses for coal;
4   legislation to facilitate the development of the Selby coalfield and to promote expanding production of opencast coal.

Drawing lessons from recent history, the government also undertook to be prepared to act financially if public policies prevented commercial pricing (soon overtaken by the announcement of policies intended deliberately to make fuels expensive), or if there were troubles due to short-term variations in the prices of competing fuel. Assistance was also promised where certain coal products might be essential to the national interest. Yet, far from being a licence for featherbedding, the Report showed a clear understanding of commercial realities, seeing an assured long-term future for an efficient competitive coal industry. Consequently all parties saw the importance of a sound and effective production incentive scheme. (In fact, there had already been a series of earlier meetings of a joint NCB/NUM working party discussing possible incentive schemes.) Though the spur nationally was meeting the energy needs and reducing the burden on the balance of payments of imported fuels, the great opportunities were for 'competitive coal'. So the Board and the NUM were to

work out as soon as possible an effective and viable incentive scheme for the industry which fairly and justly rewards extra effort wherever it is applied and which will lead to a rapid increase in supplies to meet the demands of customers. The first essential is to satisfy and hold the industry's present markets.

On the central issue of development plans, the government endorsed the general strategy of the NCB set out in its *Plan for Coal.* Each coalfield would share in major investment to provide 42 million tons of new capacity by 1985 by extending the life of existing pits, increasing the output at existing pits by major projects and by opening new collieries. Twenty major schemes had already been set in progress. Planning had begun to exploit the extensive Barnsley Seam reserves near Selby in Yorkshire (discussed in more detail in the following chapter). Over the ten-year period an additional investment of £600 million was authorised on top of an earlier £800 million already planned to maintain annual deep-mined output of at least 120 million tons and if possible to increase it, with a large contribution from opencast working which was due to rise from 10 million to 15 million tons a year.

Good prospects for the long-term future of the industry were seen as linked with the proposals for research and development of new uses for coal which would be most economically and effectively carried out by co-operation and involvement of those due to benefit – prospective customers, process plant manufacturers and workers in other countries with whom there could be mutually helpful interchanges.

To achieve great efficiency and productivity with greater safety and better working conditions, mining research on established techniques and equipment was to place particular emphasis on increasing the extent of applying remote and automatic controls. A New Methods Group would study the options for 'a new generation of mining systems and technology' in view of the limits for developing existing ones. The fruits of these longer-term labours were to be gathered, it was hoped, in 1985. The guiding development committees for the mining research programmes were each chaired by area directors – a device ensuring close links so that applied research stays close to the needs of the ultimate producers and the latter feel themselves involved in the success of equipment and procedures they have helped to introduce. Separate working groups had investigated respectively Industrial Relations, Research and Development, and Demand and

Supply to provide the necessary detailed information within the terms of reference, defined as 'to consider and advise on the contribution which coal can best make to the country's energy requirements and the steps needed to secure that contribution'.

AFTER THE PRICE SHOCK

In the first full year after the major oil price rises, the output at 115 million tons was assessed by the Board as roughly at the same level as would have been reached in the previous year if there had been no dispute. In a year of extraordinary wage inflation in industry in general, the Board agreed a 23½ per cent increase in miners' basic earnings, increased prices (cautiously retaining an advantage over oil), and made an operating profit of £33·8 million which covered its commitments despite a reduction of £61·9 million in government grants and a special contribution by the Board to pneumoconiosis compensation. (The reduced grants, totalling £68·2 million, included £13·8 million for social costs such as those involved in redeploying Board employees and eliminating uneconomic colliery capacity, and a regional grant of £37·8 million presumably similar to those made to private industry.) The total number of mineworkers increased during the year for the first time since 1957. The industry had again passed through a turning-point – this time, a trough – and was beginning to grow. But mining is a trade where recruiting new forces means a major training effort, and it was only towards the end of the year that more manpower was available for productive work. Overall productivity recovered only to figures below those of two years earlier, but towards the end of the year new records were being set for daily output per face and output per face manshift. But the negotiations on a productivity scheme ran into difficulties. The NCB favoured one based on norms appropriate to the conditions of each coalface. Though this was for a bonus, not for basic pay, it still ran athwart the widespread 'egalitarian' feeling of miners that many social investigators had noted. It was rejected by NUM members in a ballot. Later in the year, an alternative scheme based on total national output was agreed as part of general wage negotiations; so far it has not proved very effective.

As the industry now stands poised for a recovery which will call for a major effort in its first investment programme for over fifteen years intended actually to expand its output, as distinct from those intended to control the rate of run-down in a pattern of improved efficiency, it is interesting to compare and contrast it with the aggregation of pits in 1947 that the newly appointed Board was striving to weld into a national organisation. That cross-sectional view formed the subject of Chapter 4.

Here we move on to examine where the industry stood in mid-1975.

SUGGESTED FURTHER READING

Fuel Policy Cmnd 3438 (HMSO, 1967)

Energy in Europe: The importance of coal, a report by CEPCEO (Association of the Coal Producers of the European Community, 1974)

'The changing energy situation', *Economic Progress Report,* No. 50 (May 1974)

'Trade with OPEC Countries' and 'Saving Energy'. Both in *Economic Progress Report,* No. 64 (July 1975)

National Coal Board, *Annual Reports and Statements of Account* 1973/74, 1974/75.

Annual Reports of Conference of the National Union of Mineworkers 1973, 1974

Geoffrey Chandler 'Energy – the international compulsions', *Coal and Energy Quarterly,* No. 1 (Summer 1974)

The Relative Pay of Mineworkers, Cmnd 5567 (HMSO, 1974)

Coal Industry Examination: Final Report 1974 (Department of Energy)

CHAPTER 11

Coal industry 1975/76

When the packing operation is successfully mechanised the last stronghold of the miner's shovel will have disappeared
> Article on 'Mechanisation' by Sir Andrew Bryan, former Chief Inspector of Mines, former NCB member

Over the time-span of a generation the coal industry has been transformed from one based wholly on heavy, manual work to a mechanised set of activities demanding the skills of the technical tradesman allied to the traditional knowledge of the miner. About 800 separate organisations owning some 1,000 pits had by the spring of 1976 become one nationalised body working only 241 producing units. Since 1947 manpower had fallen from 711,000 to 247,100 but deep-mined output has dropped far less, thanks to large improvements in productivity. Defined in terms of cwt output per manshift (o.m.s.), productivity has more than doubled from 21·5 to 44·8 with even bigger gains in the figures for o.m.s. at the face – 58·4 rose to 155·4. Change in output per man-year was not as great, owing to the smaller number of shifts worked and also presumably to a higher absence rate, up by a third despite all efforts and appears to stem this feature which adds to the difficulty of organising production. Overall, annual deep-mined output has consequently fallen from 184·4 million tons, through a peak in the expanding years, to 112·6 million tons. Mechanisation has both lightened the work and made it more productive; at the time of nationalisation only 2·4 per cent of the output was listed as 'mechanised' (the pioneer of cutter-loaders, the AB Meco-Moore machine, was first put to work on a longwall face in 1943); by 1976 93·6 per cent was obtained wholly mechanically. The newer methods saved lives, too. No fewer than 618 men were killed in the first year after the mines were taken over, while the toll in 1974–5 with about one-third the manpower, was 59 – every one still a reproach, but the change indicating the concern of the Board to reduce this terrible waste of life.

MECHANISATION

How have these improvements been achieved? Sir Andrew Bryan, a former Chief Inspector of Mines, points out in an article that weaves together human and organisational aspects with the purely technical, that mechanisation alone is not enough. He concludes 'As R. H. Tawney so well said, "Unless industry is to be paralysed by recurrent revolts on the part of outraged human nature, it must satisfy criteria that are not purely economic".' From an early stage, reports Sir Andrew, the Board realised the importance of short intensive courses of instruction dealing not only with seam conditions, transport of coal from working face to wagon, and the like, but also with the effects on the men at the face, officials and craftsmen, training of staff and workmen, monitoring what a new method actually achieved. Instruction was given to all ranks on a scale claimed to be without parallel at its time in other industries. It was closer than formal 'consultation', for it was a process of 'intimate communication through detailed explanation and discussion of projects'.

In purely technical terms, the arrangements evolved through a series of stages of trials towards the target of working with a longwall face where the front was free of props so that the cutter-loader could travel without obstruction and then an armoured flexible conveyor could be advanced without hindrance after a 'slice' of coal had been cut and loaded, very close behind the cutting machine. In turn this meant that roof supports could be advanced immediately behind the cutting machine, giving prompt support to the newly exposed roof. Strong and flexible support was

Fig. 8   A ranging drum shearer at Hucknall Colliery. (NCB.)

given by powered systems for holding up the roof which were also powered to be self-advancing, further reducing the need for heavy physical effort. This combination of devices brought simultaneous advances in productivity and safety. It also led to extending the practice of totally 'caving', that is collapsing the waste area left behind after the coal had been extracted in place of 'strip packing' it. (In this sense 'packing' means building by hand a 'pack' of stone to support the roof in the waste area.) This further contributed to improved safety. The resulting 'dramatic reduction in accidents from falls of ground at the working face' is shown in Table 13.

Table 13   *Persons killed and seriously injured by falls of ground at the working face and rate per 100,000 manshifts worked*

Year	Killed	Rate	Seriously injured	Rate
1947	187	0·14	845	0·64
1950	146	0·12	641	0·49
1955	160	0·12	607	0·45
1960	108	0·10	593	0·56
1965	70	0·09	380	0·48
1967/70	18	0·03	155	0·31
1973/74	14	0·04	81	0·22

Now the problems are those of complete integration and remote control, eliminating men from the face except when machines are being installed, maintained or inspected.

But Sir Andrew has also shrewdly commented on some of the consequences in man-management such as providing incentives, choosing suitable methods of payment, providing suitable supervision. For the older cycles of work provided some degree of compulsion to get each stage of the tasks completed on time so that the next one could continue. Modern faces allow work to be stopped at any time without the same urge to complete a specific task by a given time. His comments were made before difficulties had emerged in the inadequate results of the national production bonus and point to the need for fresh ideas for incentives which are fair to all concerned – but also get results.

How can further radical improvements in mining productivity now be achieved? Mr P. G. Tregelles, Director of Mining Research and Development, has said that he sees no innovation in mining techniques that will have an effect in the next ten years comparable with that resulting from introducing powered supports. The clue to progress is likely to lie in finding ways of utilising much more fully existing plant and resources which are at present grossly under-utilised. For this, the two causes are analysed as being inadequate reliability and difficulties in control of complex operations. So, the solutions are seen as lying very greatly in developing control technology, using relevant experience and developments from other industries. This technology is defined as an extension of control engineering where equipment performs with self-regulation in a control cycle (measuring differences between actual and required performance, feeding back a signal to control equipment which then takes automatic action to correct the error). Modern control technology is claimed to embrace large systems which will include many machines and will involve both men and management. With this must proceed work on improving engineering reliability in complex systems by studying and re-designing the parts to ensure that they meet the objectives of the system. Progress on these lines is needed to ensure the success of remote and automatic control of existing mining systems. Taking account of the human problems, the researchers intend to introduce the new technology 'in an evolutionary manner' through modest schemes covering particular activities such as environmental monitoring and coal preparation (size-grading coal and reducing its ash content). Their aim is to have the advantages appreciated and welcomed so that 'the changes in management style that will be required are absorbed naturally and with confidence'. Detailed research programmes are related to this strategy. A new one of special interest is on ergonomics – broadly designing and using machines in ways connected with the capabilities and sizes of men and not simply based on technical criteria – are part of a set of medical researches in collaboration with the EEC and financially supported by that body.

More generally, a pattern is growing of active international collaboration which includes that of the development committees in mining research (briefly mentioned earlier). The committees control project groups working on these topics :

1   improving the reliability of the coalface machinery and the working system;
2   increasing the tonnage of coal won for each pass of the cutter-loader machine through the face;
3   creating a family of machines to speed the driving of roadways over the full range of circumstances of height, distance and hardness of strata;
4   developing the capacity of conveyor systems to deal with surges of output from higher-capacity coalface equipment;
5   developing new systems of transport for men and materials – fast, reliable, with high weight capacity;
6   rationalising coal preparation plants, developing systems for automatically controlling the process;
7   comprehensive monitoring – collecting and transmitting information, appraising, integrating and reporting it to management as part of developing the precursors for remote and automatic control;
8   basic studies to extend fundamental knowledge of mining conditions and to survey other scientific activities for materials or concepts of value;
9   extending testing before new equipment is widely introduced, developing specifications, assessing proprietary equipment, investigating failures in service.

Staff and facilities have been greatly expanded in the last year or two to speed up this work. An offshoot of the collaboration with manufacturers of mining equipment that it entails, is that export sales of this equipment are booming in the new turn to coal on a world scale.

MARKETS, CURRENT AND FUTURE

In 1974–5 sales of coal increased to almost every class of consumer over those of the previous year, although total inland energy consumption had fallen as a result of the combined effects of industrial recession, energy conservation measures and sharp rises in prices. Power stations continued to provide more than half the market for coal (71 million tons out of 125 total inland), but coal had ceased to be the 'residual' fuel chosen only when there were difficulties in getting others. Nevertheless, Mr Arthur Hawkins, Chairman of the Central Electricity Generating Board (CEGB), complained, not for the first time, about the enormous financial burden placed upon the Board in this case by the average 70 per cent increase in fuel cost during the year (including a much larger one from coal), though he acknowledged that coal from most pits was now cheaper than fuel oil.

Sales to industry – running at a level comparable with those of 1972–3 – had stopped falling and the Board reported that an increased number of customers were looking to new coal-fired plant. Local authorities began to show interest in group heating from solid fuel. For the index of relative prices cited in Chapter 7 had turned, with its implications for coal having again passed a nadir in its fortunes. Though there were local variations, the averaged estimates for prices on a comparable basis were now as shown in Table 14.

Table 14 *Fuel for power stations*

| | Pence per therm | | Coal price/ | Oil price/ |
Year	Coal	Oil	Oil price	Coal price
1972	2·9	2·5	1·16	0·86
1973	3·0	2·9	1·03	0·97
1974	4·2	6·9	0·61	1·64
1975	6·7	8·5	0·79	1·27

There were changes in prices during 1973 and 1974 so that the figures for those years are averages, while those for 1975 apply to the earlier part of the year. In addition, handling costs are higher for coal than for oil; this slightly reduces the advantage for coal but still leaves it in a favourable position for winning back markets from oil. For very big customers like CEGB or British Steel an ingenious system giving great economies in transport costs is based on rapid loading and discharge of continuously coupled trains which do not need to stop and are called 'merry-go-round' trains. Offering practical advantages to large customers, it is likely that the system will be extended. Sales both of domestic fuel and of appliances for the home increased. For coking coals – representing almost a sixth of all coal consumption – the situation was complicated; although over the year demand rose a little, it was falling towards the end of the year as a result of the low level of steel production.

There was a setback in the year 1975/76 at the (presumed) bottom of the economic recession, which hit all coal markets except the power stations – where further cuts were made in the quantity of oil burned so that coal consumption actually rose. Broadly, the difficult market conditions in that year were considered a transient feature since total energy demand fell and coal continued to be materially cheaper than oil. Thus it was expected that as the economy recovered and with it energy demand, sales of coal would again begin to rise.

On a longer-term view, markets will depend on the results of researches on coal processing and utilisation. Behind the approval by the government of the £40 million national development programme on coal conversion processes over the next five years (following the tripartite examination) was the realisation that the gas now freely flowing in and the oil due to follow shortly have relatively small reserves, so that their supplies will be falling within a couple of decades. Nuclear power was seen as contributing largely electricity during the remainder of this century, with perhaps a little process heat. It would not therefore have a significant effect on the continuing demand for the fossil fuels, coal, oil and natural gas, in the decades ahead. Of these fossil fuels coal had the natural potential long-term advantage of far larger reserves. At this stage it needs expensive processing to convert it into the more convenient liquid gaseous fuels. But consumers prefer their fuels in these convenient forms and so coal methods have to be developed to produce the coal-based substitutes at prices that will remain 'attractive' compared with those of gas and oil products. Projects devoted largely to meeting these needs are :

1   coal liquefaction by both liquid solvents and by methods using gases under very high pressures and raised temperatures (the so-called 'super-critical' condition);
2   gasifying coal with limited oxygen to yield gas suitable for synthesis;

3 gasifying coal with air to yield a fuel gas of low calorific value;

4 pyrolysis, using modern techniques.

To improve the use of coal as a fuel for power stations, the NCB has for several years devoted a substantial effort to combustion in a so-called fluidised bed – where the coal in fine particles burns on a hot bed of ash kept in continuous agitation by air blown through it, so that it behaves as a virtual liquid. Burning the coal in this way in a steam-raising boiler is calculated to be very much cheaper than existing methods and to give advantages in availability, flexibility towards fuels, atmospheric pollution control, and the possibility of improving thermal efficiency by using it with combined gas and steam turbine power plants. One early application in Britain will be in burning wastes of low calorific value, such as some colliery spoil, for raising steam. The fluidised bed can also be made to 'fix' sulphur and nitrogen oxides, which proved to be of great interest to American organisations troubled by difficulties in working within their clean air legislation. This project has attracted attention from the National Research and Development Corporation (NRDC) and the British Overseas Trade Board (BOTB) and other government departments for its overseas market prospects. Fully proving the system meant building a larger demonstration and experimental facility to resolve some key engineering uncertainties, and enable Britain to exploit its current lead in an engineering field that could have substantial international significance. After much lobbying, it was announced in mid-1976 that the International Energy Agency, Coal Technology Group, had approved construction of an 85 MW. plant at Grimethorpe Colliery. It is also US interest in power generating and displacing oil or natural gas that is at the root of the work on producing a gas of low calorific value (known as the 'low Btu gas').

Since it is widely felt that the USA will be the first country to operate the new coal conversion processes, and since it has by far the largest relevant research programme in the world, the NCB has signed an agreement with the US Department of the Interior for extensive exchange of research information as part of the pattern of international collaboration already quoted. In the International Energy Agency of sixteen major industrial nations – set up as a result of the oil crisis – the UK leads coal research and development with the NCB Board Member for Science, Mr L. Grainger, as chairman of the working party on coal technology.

Serving many of these activities is the operational research team, setting up mathematical models for forecasting demand, and aiding strategic planning by answering a series of questions on consequences in the event of particular events developing in respect of, for example, the pattern of supply of energy (in the jargon phrase, models and sub-models for a variety of scenarios). Pricing policies are also examined by these methods to determine the probable changes in demand for coal and therefore the alteration to revenue to be expected from a change in the price of coal, or the effectiveness of differential prices between summer and winter, taking into account the cost of stocking coal.

HEALTH, SAFETY, WELFARE

One of the unexpected, yet logical, consequences of the intensive drive for mechanisation has been a suggestion by Dr John S. McLintock, the NCB Chief Medical Officer, that since mining has become less arduous, the standards for fitness could be relaxed, including those for vision now that illumination underground has improved, and that the changes could be permitted without additional risk to the individuals. In recent years between 30,000 and 40,000 medical examinations have been made each year. These cover new entrants, re-examination of juveniles, rescue men and others. For men in the industry, the medical service pays particular attention to the prevalence of pneumoconiosis; increased mechanisation is acknowledged as having increased the problems of dust control engineers, but they are thought to have made progress in dealing with dust. X-ray results on men showed 'a substantial improvement' in 1975 after a number of years without any significant improvements in the prevalence of this disease in employed miners. Protection from health hazards by doctors, nurses, full-time and part-time medical centre attendants, and radiographers also covers other prescribed diseases such as beat knee, beat elbow, beat hand, dermatitis and nystagmus (for which only one case was reported in recent years); health workers also keep an eye on possibilities of harm by other causes such as noise, or – for geologists – by ionising radiations from prospecting devices.

In 1959 the Board started a periodic X-ray scheme to provide full-sized chest X-rays at collieries at five-year intervals, the interval being changed by law in 1975 to four year. During these examinations film readers also look for any other pathological condition needing attention, such as pulmonary tuberculosis, early carcinoma or cardiac abnormalities. In the pits 45,000 selected workmen and officials have been given courses on dust control, and a technical committee advises on the most efficient equipment to use on underground machines, to meet the needs of new regulations, which set out strict maximum 'permitted' dust levels.

Though the welcome fall in the death toll has been mentioned earlier, the rate for reportable accidents rose in 1974/75. Analyses of accidents show that the rate per 100,000 manshifts for fatal accidents underground away from the face has not been improving recently and that on the surface the rate for serious injuries has actually risen. Mr J. W. Calder, the former Chief Inspector of Mines, was very critical of both the failure here and the lack of progress in reducing accidents in haulage and transport. A special steering committee has been set up with representatives from the NCB, the inspectors and the Safety in Mines Research Establishment to improve safety standards of existing haulage systems and in new installations. A Safety Branch in the Mining Department with safety specialists at all levels of the organisation generally deals with these problems and publishing reports with detailed analyses. Among its activities have been the devising of pre-start warnings for power loaders, conveyors and other equipment, the running of courses for fire officers, improvements in self-rescue equipment, the running of competitions for safety and tidiness (generally linked with safety), and the promotion of publicity including films. In addition, the Coal Industry National Consultative Council, drew up a specification for the reduction of surface accidents – circulated to all levels of the industry, including colliery and workshop consultative committees.

A large part of the functions of the scientific control departments – who also have major responsibility to production and prospecting for analysing coal, water and coke – are devoted to health and safety. All working places underground are surveyed for airborne dust and some of these dusts are further examined for quartz content. The 'self-rescuers' (respirators to be carried by everyone going underground) are regularly checked and mine air analysed. The gas testing instruments may be carried to the location or the gas may in some cases be drawn through tubes to a central gas analyser; research is now in progress on automatic monitoring instruments left in position and sending signals to a central recorder. To minimise fire risk, mining materials are tested for their resistance to fire, the most thorough of the procedures being tests in real fires in tunnels called galleries. The only dust that is welcomed underground is that of limestone, used to treat roadways to prevent explosions from propagating along them; this dust must be checked for its content of quartz and the dust in the roadways for combustible matter. Scientific control laboratories carry out the testing, often service and calibrate the instruments, and carry out research to improve accuracy and productivity in analysis.

Turning to housing, where the Board at one stage accepted the need to organise building through a subsidiary organisation, there has been a change in policy. For several years now the Board has virtually ceased to build houses and has asked local authorities to provide for mineworkers where this was necessary. Overall it added 24,000 houses to the stock of 140,000 it took over on nationalisation, but it is now generally disposing of houses at the rate of about 5,000 a year up to mid-1976. Its policy is to offer them, in order of priority, to local authority, housing association, sitting tenant, and general sale. However, the Board has continued with a housing improvement programme, still owns some houses provided –

by past agreement – rent-free and maintains some houses due for demolition as soon as alternative accommodation is made available. The net cost to the Board is over £5 million a year. These houses are in effect tied, but retired miners, widows and other special cases in practice occupy about half of them. In August 1976 the remaining tenants – numbering about 85,000 – were given the option of buying their houses at about half the current market value.

Though conditions vary greatly, some pits are liable to be uncomfortably hot. There has been concern at the high temperatures encountered at greater depths that are being aggravated by the heat discharged by heavy duty machinery. Early in 1975 a large air-cooling machine was therefore installed at Bevercotes Colliery in an underground roadway. It extracts heat from the mine atmosphere and blows cool air into the ventilation system. Welcomed by the NUM, it is due to be extended, if the trials go well, first into other working places in Bevercotes, with the implication that similar machines will go to other places where excessive heat causes difficulties.

A wider-ranging advance in conditions is in providing pensions. At nationalisation there were no pension schemes for miners. From 1952, the NCB introduced a flat-rate pension scheme, but this was replaced in April 1975 by one negotiated with the NUM which is earnings-related, providing improved benefits, with increases in lump sum payments and widows' benefits.

CARE FOR THE ENVIRONMENT

As part of the new plans, opencast coal is due to supply up to 15 million tons a year (the present contribution being about 10 million). Overall, the NCB, using contractors, has produced well over 150 million tons by this means, providing both cheaper coal and higher profits. Techniques have been worked out to keep separate topsoil, subsoil and the rest of the excavated earth, while mounds are formed to minimise noise to neighbouring districts. The soils are replaced to suitable contours and the Ministry of Agriculture manages the land on the Board's behalf for five years. After many years of complaints – some justified, many exaggerated – the Board is sensitive on the issue and emphasises its great concern to reduce nuisance, to combine reclamation schemes for pit heaps and other derelict land with opencast mining, and to restore farmland and fences, gates and buildings to high standards.

To dispose of colliery tips, the NCB set up a Minestone Executive which is succeeding in having the colliery shale used in roadworks. It is largely clay mineral with small amounts of pyrite, carbonates and quartz; in older tips there may have been some spontaneous combustion and the residue is known as burnt shale. Both are usable and the Department of the Environment, after testing by its engineers, has encouraged their use. Contractors needing fill material for earthworks are invited to tender on a dual basis; one price is based on their finding fill material in the normal way and the other is for material from a specified site such as a colliery tip. The choice of tender is then made not purely on price but also taking into account environmental considerations. This removes the pit heaps and avoids the need to create further dereliction by taking fill out of 'borrow pits' damaging the landscape. Minestone has now been built into many trunk roads and motorways. Elsewhere, in co-operation with county authorities the Board has treated a pit heap to help restore a nature reserve and bird sanctuary, tipped in an agreed way to create a golf course, tipped to create other agreed landscape patterns and provided a base for playing fields. At Pegwell Bay, Kent, colliery shale was the foundation for a Hoverport.

Heat-treated, minestone may be used as an aggregate for making concrete. The Building Research Establishment has examined possible uses with and without heat treatment for this purpose and has gone on to consider other applications, such as making skid-resistant roadstone, bricks and Portland cement where the minestone would replace clay. Many of these ideas combine possibilities of improving the environment around collieries – often left in a depressing state over decades of neglect – and of financial benefit to the Board, achieving the remarkable feat of combining social virtue with profit.

In and around collieries and villages the NCB continues efforts to brighten up the environment, rehabilitate the surface areas of the mines and improve graphic design, for example by a 'House Style' for notices, sign posts, road vehicles and so on. In 1974–75 it reported that it had also 'contributed to the activities of the Business and Industry Panel of European Architectural Heritage Year 1975, and have taken steps to identify and record items of interest in the heritage of the industry through industrial museums and preservation societies, in conjunction with the Department of the Environment and local authorities'. In particular, the NCB has now adopted a policy of preserving some industrial relics and a national museum is being built up at Lound Hall in Nottinghamshire, near Bevercotes Colliery. Jointly with other bodies it is running competitions for the tidiest pit village and the tidiest pit top, a project that will also contribute to safety.

ANCILLARIES

Under this heading are grouped the manufacture of smokeless fuels, undersea exploration and exploiting of gas from the North Sea, exploring for oil (though the North Sea activities are likely to be transferred to the British National Oil Corporation) and chemical manufacture. Branching well beyond the traditional gasworks recovery of chemicals from coal carbonisation, the Board through its subsidiary companies and partnerships makes a silicone injection damp-proof course, modified PVC with a useful heat-shrink property, and cheaper epoxy resins for adhesives and floorings, in addition to the caprolactam (for nylon) that came from Nypro. This group of enterprises contributed almost £23 million to profits in 1974–75, and forms a company called NCB (Coal Products) Ltd.

A further subsidiary, NCB (Ancillaries) Ltd, manages the solid fuel distribution interests, the computer company Compower Ltd, companies running engineering and estates activities, brickmaking, mining consultancy services and others. Several of these, including the consultancy, are part-owned. The company was able to turn in an increased profit of £9·1 million to its owners in the 1975/76 accounts. Broadly these enterprising developments – excluding the special case of the major disaster at Nypro – have tended to expand and to improve in profitability.

It is likely that some of the research projects mentioned earlier will lead to chemical products as well as yielding refined fuels. Longer-term, super-critical gas extraction may be able to offer this type of high-value product from coal. Extracting with anthracene oil is already resulting in a very pure electrode coke suitable for arc steel furnaces. Over a six-month period, Mr J. McLaren and his colleagues at the Stoke Orchard Research Establishment made some thirty tons, accepted on experimental trials and due to go forward for commercial scale tests. With British Steel and other possible collaborators, the NCB has made feasibility studies for making chemicals on a large scale, originally to use their expected North Sea crude oil to made petrochemicals which now dominate the market for the important group known as 'aromatic' chemicals and their derivatives – but also as a 'precursor of a new coal based chemical industry'. As a distant vision, the researchers have put forward the concept of a 'coalplex' – a complex of activities that may combine manufacture of chemicals and of electricity, using by various schemes of district or group heating the heat at present wasted, and all based on coal. Well before that stage it seems likely that a group of chemical processes will send on to the markets improvements in a binder for coke, new plastics, active carbon (for recovering solvent or for respirators), mastics, as well as offering the residue from the solvent extraction as a high ash solid fuel.

RECRUITS AND TRAINING

The new wave of recruiting has not only added manpower but has rejuvenated, in some degree, the mining labour force; at the end of 1975 the average age at 43·2 was the lowest since 1964. For young newcomers, the coal industry offers student apprenticeships in several branches of engineering, taking the students up to various levels of qualification according to interest and ability, and others for engineering draughtsmen. University graduates can gain scholarships for engineering including chemical engineering, leading on to further training as a stepping-stone to management posts. For the skilled general run of mining jobs, the intake between 16 and 18 receive six months of training, taking them in stages to full underground work. Those going forward to become fitters, electricians or other engineering craftsmen have their own apprenticeship schemes which can extend for four years. The other specialists for such areas as industrial relations, marketing, finance, general clerical duties, and secretaries, similarly have equivalent facilities, and juniors entering laboratories are encouraged to study for higher qualifications.

The new expansion phase means that older recruits are also being accepted for a range of trades within the pits and above ground, including opportunities for graduates. Obviously recruitment is likely to be favoured by the interaction of better wages, growing confidence in the future of mining as a career, and the highest rate of general unemployment since the Second World War. One colliery, in a district not outstandingly hard hit by unemployment, reported in mid-1975 that for the first time for some twenty years it had twice as many recruits as it could handle and accept.

DEVELOPMENT

'This new situation, in fact, heralds a new era in the energy scene – the second coming of coal.' But Mr G. Armstrong, of the Coal Department of British Petroleum Ltd, making this assessment in an address to the British Association in 1974 also added that it might not endure at a high level of utilisation for much more than the next twenty-five years, bridging the transitional period before nuclear power becomes our main source of energy. Any major extensions were seen as due to using coal for liquefaction and gasification rather than as a direct source of heat.

Nevertheless, where the future for fossil fuel lies is evident from the fact that, in the USA, oil companies have now taken a financial interest in well over half of the American coal reserves. A large part of the exploration for coal around

Fig. 9   The mouth of New Drift at Silverdale Colliery. (NCB.)

the world is now due to the oil companies, and the engagement by BP of Mr Armstrong, a former Chief Geologist of the NCB, with others from the same source, is highly significant of the relative reserves of petroleum and of coal on a world scale.

In Britain intensive exploration by the NCB in the last four years has greatly increased proven economically recoverable reserves, notably in Yorkshire and Nottinghamshire. Undoubtedly, the brightest of these new jewels is the Selby coalfield where reserves in one seam alone – the Barnsley seam – are estimated to be sufficient to supply a yearly output of 10 million tons into the next century. Thus this project will provide almost a quarter of the 42 million tons a year of new capacity to be created by the mid-1980s. How will this affect the environment in the mainly rural area between Selby and York? Planning has been based on bringing out this enormous quantity of coal through a pair of sloping tunnels – known as drifts – on massive conveyor belts; the outlet will be in a disused railway marshalling yard and consequently will introduce no fresh despoliation. All the coal is destined for power stations, and is due to be transported by the permanently-coupled liner trains. Other details announced include an undertaking that associated shafts,

> situated at five sites in the Plain of York, would be used only for ventilation, materials handling and manriding, and the sites would be landscaped. No coal would come to the surface at these sites once the complex was in co-ordinated operation . . . maximum use to be made of automation and remote control techniques, including the use of computers programmed to react to changes in coal flow.

As a result, an output normally needing at least five modern collieries if worked by conventional methods and probably 20,000 men, will emerge from one outlet point and require about 4,000 men. As one would expect, the Board makes pious declarations about its consciousness of its responsibility to protect the environment. But favourable geological conditions do really seem to enable it to plan extraordinary output and productivity with remarkable little disturbance to the neighbourhood. The ancient abbey in the centre of the town of Selby is also to be specifically protected; no mine workings will approach its foundations.

In his address in 1975 to the annual conference of the National Union of Mineworkers, the NCB Chairman, Sir Derek Ezra, reported vigorous action on the recommendations

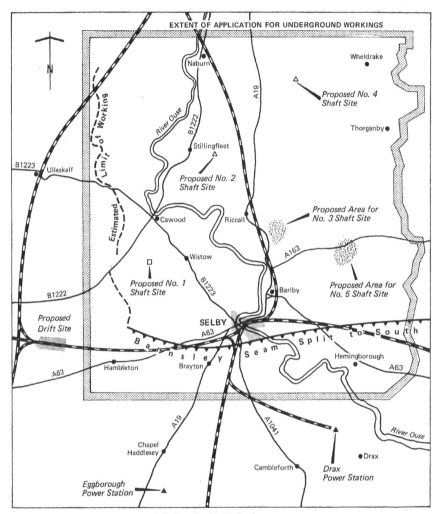

Fig. 10   A map of Selby Coalfield Project.

of the Final Report of the Tripartite Coal Industry Examination. Included were information on :

1   the results of the exploration efforts, 'now adding to our economically recoverable reserves at an annual rate of 500 million tons'.
2   projects costing £110 million approved and due to initiate 9 million tons of new capacity. The approval of the Selby project would mean that over half of the 42 million tons new capacity would have been initiated;
3   new drift mines at Bettws in South Wales and Royston in Barnsley and preliminary investigations for new mines at Park in Staffordshire and south of the present Notts coalfield.

Dimming the glowing prospects from these developments was the current low level of output, 'throwing into question our ability to produce the tonnages envisaged . . . endangering our credibility with the nation'. Late in 1975 there was still no sign of productivity recovering from this unexpected plateau in the summer of 1975.

In assessing probable future output, the new capacity cannot, of course, simply be added to existing figures. Schumacher, it may be recalled, had earlier reckoned that 2 per cent per year of capacity, on average, was lost as a result of worked out seams or even pits; Armstrong set it a little higher, estimating the loss at 3 million tons of mining capacity a year (the figure given in the NCB's 'Plan for Coal') through exhausting reserves and probably also closures on economic grounds. Consequently, even if the full additional capacity is achieved, this is likely to mean a net gain of only about 10 million tons of capacity. Presumably the one feature that could invalidate this type of assessment would be if the new research projects for much higher utilisation of equipment enabled greater outputs to be achieved than those expected from the capacity available. I understand that the oil companies do not consider this probable, nor do they think that large amounts of coal will be produced at prices competitive with oil or with imported coal. Consequently they are preparing to import coal from other parts of the world that are able to produce it more cheaply. Whether the trends in the British coal industry are able to falsify these prognostications remains to be seen.

Officially, the NUM continues to urge full support for the productivity drive by its members. Joe Gormley, in his Presidential Address in 1975 looking 'forward with a new heart to the success of this Coal Industry', chided his members in some degree concerning the response to the new opportunities. What separated us from other countries able to pay high wages without the same degree of inflation, he said, was that their production per manshift must be far higher than in Britain. Gormley advised his conference to have a productivity scheme with targets at pit level, but the vote went against him and a national scheme was adopted. When I asked him for his views on the failure of this remote system of incentives he pointed to the pit stocks with ominous memories for miners (though they were in fact not over-large) and also the general state of the economy. Gormley continues to press his colleagues to have a scheme based on pit targets adopted by consultative procedures with all those affected, combined with a nationally negotiated system of bonus awards. The setback he attributes to the interaction of the recession and the ineffective scheme, but he looked forward to both altering in the near future.

The greatest of the differences from the industry that was taken over from its private owners is a workforce with an official leadership that is committed to its success, despite the productivity doldrums of 1975. It is the miners' own elected leader who has repeatedly scolded them for not providing value for the investment that the nation is now putting into the mines. Despite the widely publicised rogue views of some executive members, the union overwhelmingly agrees that, having demanded nationalisation, the union shares a responsibility for making it a success. Gormley claims that he sees signs that the plateau in productivity is due to lack of stimulus to the men because the economy as a whole is in recession. A lot depends on the accuracy of this interpretation. But certainly from the leadership the goodwill is there in a way that is a revolution compared with attitudes in bygone days. Now the need is for a practical demonstration that this change pervades the men in the pits.

Yet coal is now only one of the four major primary fuels. At this stage, what is the overall energy perspective?

SUGGESTED FURTHER READING

National Coal Board, *Report and Accounts* 1974/5
National Coal Board, *Statistical Tables* 1974/5
National Coal Board, *Report and Accounts* 1975/6
National Coal Board, *Statistical Tables* 1975/6
Annual Report of the Chief Safety Engineer for 1973/4 (National Coal Board, 1974)
Coal Industry Examination: Final Report 1974 (Department of Energy)
Sir Andrew Bryan, 'Mechanisation – the dream that became reality'.
Coal and Energy Quarterly, No. 4 (Spring 1975)
Norman Siddall, 'What R & D will contribute to coal's future', *Coal and Energy Quarterly,* No. 5 (Summer 1975)
John Rogers, 'Mining equipment booming in world energy crisis', *Coal and Energy Quarterly,* No. 5 (Summer 1975)
P. G. Tregelles, 'The contribution of new technology to mining systems', paper presented to the Midland Institute of Mining Engineers, March 1975
Report of HM Chief Inspector of Mines and Quarries for 1974 (HMSO, 1975)
Address by Sir Derek Ezra, Chairman of the NCB, to the Annual Conference of the NUM at Scarborough, 1975 (NCB, 1975)
G. Armstrong, 'Coal and the Energy Crisis', Sectional Presidential Address at British Association for the Advancement of Science, 1974
W. Gutt *et al., A survey of the locations, disposal and prospective uses of the major industrial by-products and waste materials.* (Watford, Building Research Establishment, 1974)
NCB Plan for Coal (NCB, 1974)
Presidential Address of J. Gormley, OBE, at the Annual Conference (NUM, 1975)

CHAPTER 12

Fuel Policies 1975/76

*There are only two qualities in the world: efficiency
and inefficiency; and only two sorts of people: the
efficient and the inefficient*
    John Bull's Other Island, by George Bernard Shaw

Though the whole economic and social structure of the industrialised world (capitalist and communist) has not come
tumbling down in the wake of the abrupt oil price rises – as
some early commentators had seemed to expect – a great network of defensive reactions was certainly set in motion
throughout the world. Governments, companies and individuals have taken measures which have included various forms
of political pressure and : .

1   a drive for economy : avoiding waste, improving insulation
    of buildings, avoiding leakages in equipment, reconsider-
    ing whether discharged heat can be recovered – as in
    thermal linkage schemes;
2   turning back to coal, now at a stroke once again made
    competitive with oil for many applications;
3   attempts to speed the contribution of nuclear energy;
4   increased prospecting for oil;
5   building stocks of oil;
6   reconsidering sources of hydrocarbon fuel previously
    thought uneconomic, notably the oil shales of the USA
    and the tar sands of Canada;
7   reconsidering energy sources previously thought unecono-
    mic or of interest only in very few situations, for example,
    geothermal, tidal, wavepower, ocean thermal currents,
    wind sources, and solar energy in temperate zones.

The previous pattern of increasing oil consumption at about 7 per cent per annum was sharply broken and oil consumption throughout the world decreased, leaving tankers idle under the combined effects of the general economic setback and the economy measures. In June 1976, it was reckoned that 16 per cent of the world tanker fleet was still lying idle. (Because of expectations based on earlier trends, the world tanker and combined carrier fleet had actually grown 18 per cent in capacity during 1974.) Estimates by Shell showing the earlier energy trend and the abrupt change are given in Table 15.

Table 15   *Estimated commercial energy consumption: World (excluding USSR/Eastern Europe/China) (million b/d of oil equivalent)*

	1964	1969	1973	1974**
Solid fuels	15·5	15·9	15·7	16·0
Petroleum fuels*	23·3	32·6	43·6	42·3
Natural gas	8·1	11·9	16·1	16·4
Hydro electricity†	4·1	5·2	5·8	6·1
Nuclear electricity†	0·1	0·3	0·9	1·3
TOTAL	51·1	65·9	82·1	82·1

*includes refinery use and loss
†input equivalent basis
**provisional figures
Source: *Oil and Gas in 1974,* Shell Briefing Service

Clearly, within a static total of energy consumption all the other fuels gained a little ground at the expense of oil. All areas of the oil-producing world responded by some slackening of expansion or even a reduction, the outstanding exceptions being Saudi Arabia with an increase of output of 11·9 per cent over 1973 (though it did in turn reduce production in 1975) and the USSR, Eastern Europe and China – grouped together in these returns – where production went up by 8 per cent. In addition to the figures in the table, about 5 million barrels/day were consumed in non-energy uses, such as chemical feedstocks, bitumen and lubricants in both 1973 and the following year.

In the USA energy consumption declined in 1974 and there was some degree of shift from imported oil to domestically produced coal. President Nixon announced a Project Independence, though a later report by the Federal Energy Administration indicated considerable scepticism about its practicability. Nevertheless, President Ford late in 1975 stated that he would ask Congress to create a $100,000 million Energy Independence Authority with the aim of making the USA 'fuel-sufficient' by 1985 (although ironically by mid-1976, US dependence on imported oil had increased and was expected to fall only a couple of years later). This included both insulation measures and a drive for new sources including 250 major new coal-mines and 150 major new coal-fired power plants. He also intended to amend clean air legislation to allow greater use of coal, striking a 'reasonable compromise on environmental concerns'. The Bureau of Mines referred to coal having a major role, calling for production to double to some 1,200 million tons annually by 1985.

Though on a much smaller scale, Canada (which is a net coal importer) expected its production of around 23 million tons of coal to grow in the future with a new programme of evaluating the coal resources available, opening both new strip and deep mines.

'As a Community response to the 1973 energy crisis', the EEC adopted as an objective the securing of guaranteed supplies of energy at prices which would not prejudice investment, economic development and the reaching of equilibria of balances of payment. To achieve this the EEC proposed a policy of increasing substantially over the next ten years the production of electricity from nuclear power, maintaining the production of coal at present levels (that is, halting the rundown previously intended), reducing imports of crude oil, and using greater supplies of gas. Financial assistance was offered from Community funds for various projects to assist in meeting the objective, and this included aid to the British coal industry. Even NATO decided that it was part of its function to set up a study on energy conservation in buildings and energy conservation in industry.

Individual countries urgently carried through appraisal of energy policy. For example, German policy was evidently greatly influenced by the findings of a survey showing that almost half the final energy was applied in the form of low temperature heat. Most of it goes for heating buildings and a smaller part for supplying hot water. (And about half of the high-value electrical energy was similarly used to produce low temperature heat, largely in homes.) Herr Hans Matthofer, Minister of Research and Technology, announced a plan to use the excess heat from atomic power stations (and other generating plant) to power a nationwide central heating system. The aim would be to save oil, and also incidentally to avoid raising the temperature of rivers. A major programme was also announced on solar energy for producing hot water. In respect of coal, the Federal Government decided to arrest the decline in output (the pattern of events in West Germany was in several respects very similar to that in Britain) and to stabilise it at its level in 1974, that is roughly 95 million tons of hard coal with a further 40 million tons of brown coal. A large programme of coal conversion research is in progress and coal interests are pressing the government to develop a policy now for meeting an expected increase in future demand for hard coal.

Poland, a further important European producer with a 1974 output of 162 million tons, plans a progressive build-up to 200 million tons in 1980.

IN THE UK

The years since 1973 have seen a spate of economic and technical seminars, conferences and reports on improving fuel efficiency and on conserving energy in the UK. For the first time, a report by the Central Policy Review Staff – the so-called 'Think-Tank' – was openly published, since it dealt with energy conservation. On the same day the National Economic Development Office published results of studies on the implications for UK industry of the increased cost of energy, followed a few months later by its own assessment on energy conservation. The combined effects of propaganda, higher prices and industrial recession were a fall in inland energy consumption from 346·1 million tons equivalent in 1973 to 331·0 the following year. The fall was considered to be real, even though figures from November 1973 to March 1974 were progressively more and more affected by the miners' overtime ban, then the strike and the restrictions on fuel use. Within these figures, gas and nuclear electricity showed increases in consumption while coal and oil bore the losses. Overall the inland consumption of energy in 1974 was reported in million tons coal equivalent on the basis of primary fuel input as:

Coal	115·9
Petroleum	149·0
Natural gas	52·1
Nuclear electricity	11·9
Hydro electricity	2·1
TOTAL	331·0

So important was energy conservation rated that it was a major feature of the autumn 1974 Budget. Mr Dennis Healey, the Chancellor, said that Britain was going to be forced to alter its behaviour in response to the enormous increases in the cost of energy; then he proceeded to add to them. Subsidies to nationalised industries were to be phased out, affecting electricity, gas and coal prices, causing them to rise to 'realistic' levels. His aim was to reduce demand because it was imported oil that was used to produce electricity for satisfying extra demand. Initial allowance for expenditure on insulating industrial buildings was raised to 100 per cent (though no similar direct incentive was given to householders) and the VAT on petrol was increased to 25 per cent.

Shortly afterwards, Mr Eric Varley, then Secretary of State for Energy, followed up with a twelve-point programme of measures to save energy. He had already set up an Energy Technology Support Unit for special studies of new sources and of conservation and a network of advisory and consultative committees. Internationally, the UK became a founder-member of the International Energy Agency (IEA) with a programme intended to secure oil supplies in emergency situations, and to build up co-operation among consumers and between consumers and producers; a further objective (does it conflict with the last one?) was to reduce dependence on imported oil. By mid-1975 IEA had seventeen members – among them the USA, Canada, Japan and eight EEC countries – with Norway as an associate member.

Challenged by the Commons Energy Resources Sub-Committee early in 1975 to provide a new general statement on 'middle-term objectives of British energy policy', Eric Varley indicated that he did not have it in mind to produce a White Paper comparable in size and complexity with the 1967 one. Nevertheless in response to requests by the Sub-Committee for written evidence, the Department prepared a number of individual memoranda setting out its policy framework and some forecasts. Government energy policy, explained the Department,

> is formulated within an integrated framework of analyses and forecasts in which alternative policy options in the energy sector are tested against each other and against a range of future uncertainties and constraints. One of the central difficulties . . . lies in the great uncertainty which surrounds most of the major variables . . . [so that] the range of possible outcomes is very wide.

The aim was therefore to explore future uncertainties systematically with particular emphasis on 'sensitivity analysis' – defining the area where judgements have to be made, the extent of interactions of components of the energy scene and the costs that could be involved. Using computer models, the Department explored thirty-two sets of conditions ('scenarios'), giving the ranges shown in Table 16.

These covered assumptions such as UK economic growth of 2·7 per cent annually and 3·3 per cent, oil price higher than that of coal and the reverse, high or low coal investment, high gas usage or conservation, and high or low nuclear development rate. A single set was then picked out and presented with some diffidence 'for illustrative purposes . . . not necessarily optimal' – yet obviously quoted since it must have been considered within all the justified reservations as a highly likely projection. This sample projection consisted of the figures shown in Table 17 based on associating a growth of energy demand at 2 per cent per annum with a GDP growth rate of 3·3 per cent on average.

Table 16   *UK energy consumption. The limits shown by the model runs in 1974*

	1972/73	1975	1980	1985	mtce* 1990
Energy uses					
Coal	128	119–133	107–154	84–199	77–196
Natural gas	34	46–48	54–87	62–109	56–68
Nuclear	10	14	25	33–44	50–106
Hydro	2	2	2	2	2
Oil	158	148–163	122–200	126–258	146–317
TOTAL ENERGY USES	332	344–349	368–391	407–441	464–505
Non-energy uses					
Oil (inc. bunkers)	25	27–32	39–44	48–56	60–68
Natural gas	4	4	6	7	6
TOTAL ALL USES	361	375–385	413–441	462–504	530–579
of which					
North Sea oil	—	8	170–238	170–255	170–255
All other fuels	361	367–377	175–271	207–334	275–409
North Sea oil as					
PERCENTAGE OF TOTAL					
FUEL REQUIREMENTS	—	2	39–58	34–55	29–48

*Million tons coal equivalent
Source: A memorandum of the Department of Energy, 1975

Table 17   *Sample projection**

	1973	1980	1985	mtce** 1990
Coal	131	130	135	150
Oil	159	145	170–180	175–225
Natural gas	40	80	80	65
Nuclear	10⎱	25	35–45	50–100
Hydro	2⎰			
TOTAL ENERGY	342	380	430	490
NON-ENERGY	30	45	55	65
TOTAL ALL USES	372	425	485	555
NORTH SEA OIL	—	170–240	170–255	170–255

*The sample projections have been rounded to the nearest 5 mtce
**mtce—million tons coal equivalent
Source: A memorandum of the Department of Energy, 1975

The projection is said to be based up to 1985 on the NCB *Plan for Coal*, but there seems to be some confusion between total and deep-mined planned output. In the plan the Board looked forward to a potential demand ranging up to 150 million tons a year and stated that it was planning 'toward the top of this market', with opencast providing 15 million tons a year. Simple subtraction gives a planned deep-mined output of 135 million which is shown by the Department of Energy as the total.

On nuclear power, the Department points out that earlier investment decisions have already determined the maximum availability up to about 1980, though it did not add that all the Advanced Gas-Cooled Reactors (AGRs) were several years behind schedule in coming into operation. (In April 1975, Mr Arthur Hawkins reported that Britain's eleven Magnox stations were generating 30 per cent of all nuclear power in the world and saving £84 million a year – though this is open to the criticisms detailed at the end of Chapter 8. These are reactors using natural uranium fuel elements in cans made of magnesium alloy; they are graphite-moderated and cooled by carbon dioxide.) The AGRs forming the second generation of reactors approved (though none is yet operating), use slightly enriched uranium dioxide fuel elements in stainless steel cans, again graphite-moderated, cooled by carbon dioxide but operating at a higher temperature. The government decided to base the next reactor programme on the Steam-Generating Heavy Water Reactor (SGHWR) – although debate on this decision was re-opened in 1976. This is again a reactor using slightly enriched uranium dioxide fuel elements, but it is moderated by heavy water and cooled by light water directly generating steam. An important feature of the official attitude to nuclear generation is the assumption that coal – as well as gas – is limited in supply, though for different reasons. In the case of gas, the reasoning is based on the need for thought about the best rate of depleting reserves, which may lead to policies of restricting consumption to uses considered especially suitable – described as 'premium uses'. But for coal, what is implied is that production will fall short.

In respect of oil, the memorandum repeats government

expectations that the North Sea will produce oil equivalent to all our domestic needs for oil through the 1980s but notes that uncertainties about reserves mean that we might once again become a large net importer by 1990. In the interim, before 1980, oil is still envisaged as 'fulfilling a balancing role', that is, making up any deficiencies in supplies from other sources, even though it will add to imports and is the most expensive and least secure in supply.

For electricity, estimates of demand are based on a growth rate of $3\frac{1}{2}$ to $4\frac{1}{2}$ per cent annually, though it is also acknowledged that demand for what is called 'bulk heating' may be damped down as a result of customers' use of other fuels, especially gas. All this implies that the Department, in agreement with unofficial forecasters, tends to assume that the present halt in rising demand for energy, including electricity, is only a temporary phenomenon. The demand curves are expected to go on rising, though they may reach particular levels a few years later than had previously been anticipated, the delay being caused by the combined effects of the economic recession and the conservation measures.

Because of this perspective and the view that the UK will be self-sufficient in the 1980s but may later begin again to depend on imports, the Department concludes that 'the trend of demand for electricity and doubts about the availability of fossil fuels (and other alternatives) on a sufficient scale point to the need for a large and increasing nuclear component in our energy supplies by the turn of the century'.

On these estimates electricity demand should double well before the year 2000 and might account for more than half of all energy consumption. This is why both the Department and the CEGB see a need for further building of generating stations despite the criticisms of protest groups such as Friends of the Earth who point to the great discrepancy between an existing output capacity of 58,523 MW at the end of 1974–5 and a demand that peaked at 40,973, while a further range of generating plants, including the four AGR stations, are under construction. The figure (Figure 11) comparing fossil fuel requirements with and without a major nuclear power programme powerfully supports the official case, although it

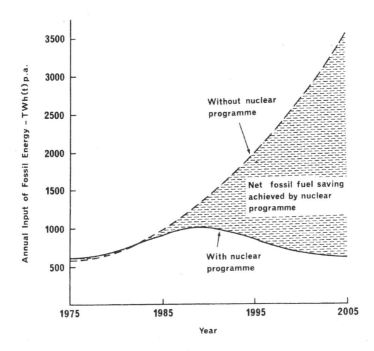

Note: 1 TWh(t) = 1 terawatt hour of energy as heat
= 1000 million kilowatt hours of heat = approximately 135 thousand tons of coal equivalent

Fig. 11   Comparison of fossil fuel requirements for building and operating power stations to meet a growth in UK electricity demand of 5 per cent per annum with and without a major nuclear power programme. (From evidence by the Department of Energy to the Study of Radiological Safety of the Royal Commission on Environmental Pollution. Reproduced by permission of the Controller of HMSO.)

appears to have been a little loaded by assuming a 5 per cent growth rate in demand for electricity in the UK while most of the narrative argument refers to a 4 per cent rate.

But by the turn of the century even world reserves of nuclear fuels will be in question if nuclear generation continues at its present low level of efficiency. Against the glowing estimates of theoretical equivalents of the energy available from the fission of uranium that were put about in the blissful dawn of nuclear enthusiasm, current commercial reactors generally extract less than 1 per cent of the potential. Consequently, the government in July 1974 announced also that it would maintain its effort on the fast reactor, expected to use uranium some sixty times more efficiently. In this the fission is caused by unmoderated high-speed electrons. A 250 MW prototype fast reactor (PFR) at Dounreay has supplied electricity to the grid and is being worked up to full power as part of an extensive development programme. In a wide-ranging memorandum (in July 1975) supplied to the Royal Commission on Environmental Pollution for its study of radiological safety, the Department of Energy also took advantage of the occasion to restate the whole argument on the part to be played by nuclear power in future energy supplies, taking a side-swipe at the safety aspects of other energy sources as well as setting out its own concern for nuclear environmental and safety issues. For coal, it commented :

> Demand [by the year 2000] could be still higher but its availability could depend on the willingness of men at that time to produce it (and the environmental consequences of mining it would not be negligible). On the other hand, demand for coal could be falling in traditional uses if other energy sources were proving more attractive.

Apart from nuclear fission, non-fission sources of energy were seen as likely to be only small contributors, so that for Britain and for the world as a whole we were forced to return to nuclear fission to fill the gap between demand and other possibilities of supply.

RESEARCH AND DEVELOPMENT (R & D)

This assessment of fuel trends for the future is strongly reflected in the relative funding of the research and development programmes, even though the Department strives to justify a policy of not considering R & D programmes on energy in terms of a total national programme. The justification given is that the programmes of the nationalised industries are formulated as integral parts of their total commercial activities, that the atomic energy research expenditure is separately voted and that 'serious interest in alternative sources of energy, such as wave power, tidal power, solar and geothermal energy, has been revived recently . . . assessments and experimental tests are now being carried out . . . and the most attractive of these options and a number of development projects are now either in progress or being given consideration'.

None of this seems to add up to a reason for not having a national R & D policy for energy, and the last argument quoted verbatim seems to be irrelevant as an objection – more valid as a supporting reason.

However, the figures shown in Table 18 are significant of a heavy commitment to nuclear energy for the future use and, despite the bold words cited above, a trivial one to the new sources. Coal, which on the basis of this no-policy approach, is left to the discretion and funding of the NCB, lies somewhere in between.

Nuclear fusion, based on effectively limitless supplies of deuterium from water and producing no pollution, is acknowledged as probably the ultimate means of providing energy 'in the very long term' and 'still the most attractive source of energy' but is funded at only £6 million a year. The Department refers to successive governments having confirmed the policy of fission reactors as our main long-term energy source, justifying the heavy expenditure in developing both the thermal reactor systems and the sodium-cooled fast reactor.

However, despite the above indications on policy-making, Mr Varley and Dr Marshall (Chief Scientist at the Department of Energy) stated in 1975 in replies to the Commons Energy Resources Sub-Committee that they did hope to be able to announce an R & D strategy when the relatively newly appointed Dr Marshall had completed his studies. Meanwhile the pattern emerging as a result of the various separate sectional strategies is shown in Table 18.

In an 'annex' to the memorandum to the Royal Commission, the Department of Energy achieves the remarkable feat of discussing the fast reactor without mentioning plutonium or 'breeding'. The PFR at Dounreay is designed to test future design features of a larger commercial fast reactor (CFR) including advanced designs of fuel. Its fuel is a mixture of uranium and plutonium compounds. A main feature of this

Table 18   *Energy research and development estimates*

R & D Area	Proposed 1975/6 Gross Expenditure £'000	
Coal		
Mining R & D	7,856	
Coal processing and combustion	2,013	
Health aspects and other	1,259	
TOTAL	11,128	
Gas		
Gas technology	6,782	
Commercial R & D and other	5,812	
TOTAL	12,594	
Electricity		
Technical R & D	35,056	
Commercial R & D	842	
TOTAL	35,898	
Nuclear (UKAEA)		
Fast reactors	31,720	
Thermal reactors	11,260	
Materials processing, waste management and active handling	7,370	
Reactor safety	8,040	
Future systems and international projects	5,560	
Contracts with nuclear industry	13,450	
TOTAL	77,400	
Offshore Technology		
Survey work	2,800	(approx)
Technological R & D	3,700	(approx)
TOTAL	6,500	
Alternative Energy Sources		
Nuclear fusion	6,000	(approx)
Wave energy	100*	(approx)
Tidal energy	(20)	(1974/75)
Wind, solar and geothermal energy, hydrogen and energy storage	400*	(approx)
TOTAL	6,500	(approx)

*£60,000 on wave energy and £30,000 on Wind, Solar, Geothermal and Energy Storage appearing here are included in the CEGB budget under ELECTRICITY, Technical R & D.

Source: A Memorandum of the Department of Energy, 1975

class of reactor is to 'breed' additional fuel; both thermal and fast reactors breed plutonium, but the fast reactors do so much more efficiently with good economy of neutrons, which are absorbed both within the core fuel and also in fertile material, in a 'breeder blanket' of uranium surrounding the core.

It is only fair to quote from Sir John Hill, chairman of the UK Atomic Energy Authority, that as far as is known no deaths have been due to radiation associated with the British nuclear power programme; both the AEA and its daughter company, British Nuclear Fuels Ltd, state that they fully understand the special precautions needed in handling and transporting plutonium. Nevertheless, this is one of the most poisonous materials known. Ten millionths of a gram are likely to cause lung cancer if inhaled and a quantity no larger than a grapefruit uniformly distributed among the world's population would be enough to poison us all. The alternative major hazard is that only 10 lb of it are needed to construct an atomic bomb. On a world scale, tens of tons are now being made each year.

In the second report of the Club of Rome, Professor M. Mesarovic and Dr E. Pestel refer to this purely technological solution of the world's energy problems as a Faustian bargain, selling our souls and those of our descendants for our immediate needs of comfort. For, on a reasonable set of assumptions about the future, including the continuing of the present growth of demand for energy, they show that in a hundred years' time the world will need 24,000 breeder reactors if we choose this method of meeting those energy needs. In turn we would need to process and transport each year 15,000 tons of plutonium. In this kind of situation, the needs of safety go far beyond technical questions of preventing losses in processing or due to accidents in transit; they also involve military issues of safeguarding against terrorists or agents of powers seeking to build bombs and political questions of damaging relations between neighbouring powers. For those not having reactors would be fearful of the military opportunities apparently available to those with them who would be handling large quantities of plutonium even if nominally for peaceful purposes. Though current quantities handled are far smaller than those in the long-range forecasts, the nature of the hazards remains. Is this a satisfactory basis for our energy policy, relying on a process that produces large quantities of what some have understandably called 'the infernal element'? Mesarovic and Pestel urge an intermediate strategy supplementing high oil usage with coal and liquefied coal since the reserves are so immense, and a long-term one based on solar energy – safe, clean, free of environmental effects, waste problems, and social and political hazards. Similar reservations and proposals have been put forward in Britain by well-informed groups including Sir Kelvin Spencer, former Chief Scientist at the Ministry of Power, and professors of engineering, building and physics, medical researchers and others.

More radical critics question assumptions that electricity consumption will continue to rise. For in Britain a report by the Building Research Establishment (BRE) has confirmed that a large part of the energy is used as low-grade heat for warming air and water, including a large proportion of electricity. In the home, for example, only 4 per cent of the net energy consumption represents the use of TV, lighting and similar duties which electricity performs uniquely or best; we might add 10 per cent for cooking where some housewives have a strong preference for using electricity. But in any case all the remainder of the energy consumption is accounted for by space and water heating. Electricity is used to supply much of these needs although only a little over a quarter of the energy supplied to the power station reaches the user, so that in logic electricity should be reserved for high-grade uses.

Thus, here as in Germany, it would be advisable to consider whether many of the needs for low-temperature heat could not be met with greater economy of energy by turning to primary sources (coal, gas, solar heat) and away from the use of electricity, which would in turn greatly reduce the future demand. Since electricity supply is publicly owned this can be contemplated as a part of national policy directly under government control. The BRE study gathers together material from many sources on the possibilities, including combined generation of heat and electricity, using heat pumps, using solar collectors, and controlling mechanical ventilation, as well as the obvious areas of heat insulation, and the examination of technical issues and economic ones on both a national scale and in terms of the individual user. Little of this is of direct comfort to the coal industry except for the strong indications of the waste in using electricity for heating which may be speeding the introduction of nuclear power unnecessarily, and the possible benefit in adopting more widespread district heating, that is heating a built-up area from a single central source, distributing the heat by a hot fluid in insulated pipes, where coal is the obvious fuel.

DEVELOPMENTS DURING 1976

It should be added that there were considerable developments in the Department of Energy during 1976 – though these did not affect the heavy commitment to nuclear energy as essential for meeting energy deficits a couple of decades ahead. Thus a discussion document issued by the Department's Advisory Council on Research and Development (ACORD), after examining a number of possible 'scenarios' of future trends, recommended priority for energy conservation, coal and nuclear technologies. These areas of technology were seen as essential over a wide range of possible conditions in the future. The document was not of course an official statement but would obviously carry considerable weight coming from a body chaired by the Department's Chief Scientist (Dr Walter Marshall, FRS) and having members drawn from oil, coal, nuclear, gas, electricity and chemical interests.

Detailed review of renewable energy resources led to the conclusion by the Energy Technology Support Unit that a successful conclusion to a vigorous programme of research and development could lead to these sources contributing the equivalent of 40 million tons of coal annually to UK energy supplies by the year 2000. Wave energy was seen as the largest likely contributor. For the period beyond 2000, it was expected that solar heating had a large potential for growth. When presenting these results, Dr Marshall added the encouraging observation that programmes could be modified in the light of new evidence and that new ideas by serious minded enthusiasts (the 'product champions' of business planning') were welcome.

The Department also issued a reply to suggestions by the Commons Select Committee on Science and Technology, for a more intensive drive on energy conservation. The government set up a Committee of Ministers to promote energy conservation, thus involving several other government departments; it also announced more help for the smaller firm to improve efficiency in using energy, extending thermal insulation requirements in building regulations and several other measures intended to achieve gains 'in a balanced way as a contribution to the efficient use of resources overall – a valid point since blinkered attention to saving fuel alone could conceivably lead to wasteful use of other resources.

But probably the most striking of the activities inaugurated by Mr Anthony Benn – who had taken over the department from Mr Varley in a government re-shuffle of responsibilities on 10 June 1975 – was holding a national energy conference in mid-1976 where he invited views from a wide range of interested parties. Going beyond the fuel interests directly concerned, they included representatives of industry, trade unions, consumers, environmental groups and others. And one of the most significant contributors was certainly Sir Brian Flowers, FRS, Chairman of the Royal Commission on Environmental Pollution who accepted the evidence on immediate safety in operating nuclear plants but expressed 'major concern' about relying on a process producing 'in quantity a by-product as dangerous as plutonium' and rejected the view that there is no alternative course of action.

SUGGESTED FURTHER READING

The Select Committee on Science and Technology (Energy Resources Sub-Committee) Minutes of Evidence. Wed. 12 March 1975. Session 1974–5 (HMSO, 1975)

Royal Commission on Environmental Pollution. *Study of Radiological Safety. Evidence by the Department of Energy* (Department of Energy, 1975)

'Saving Energy'. Article in Economic Progress Report, No. 64, July 1975

Energy Conservation. A report by the Central Policy Review Staff (HMSO, 1974)

The increased cost of energy – implications for UK industry. National Economic Development Office (HMSO 1974)

Energy Conservation in the United Kingdom. National Economic Development Office (HMSO, 1975)

Oil and gas in 1974. Shell Briefing Service. (London and Rotterdam, Shell, 1975)

Energy Conservation: a study of energy consumption in buildings and possible means of saving energy in housing. A BRE Working Party Report. (Building Research Establishment, 1975)

Coal and Energy Quarterly, No 6 (Autumn 1975) contains several relevant articles on nuclear power, progress on 'Plan for Coal', North Sea oil and on the contribution that can be made by engineers to energy efficiency

Letter in *The Guardian* 7 January 1975, from Professor D. Bryce Smith and others. 'Nuclear Dustline for the Centuries'

Energy R & D in the United Kingdom. A discussion document prepared for the Advisory Council on Research and Development for Fuel and Power. Department of Energy 1976

Energy Conservation. The government's reply to the First Report from the Select Committee on Science and Technology, Session 1974–5. HMSO Cmnd 6575, 1976

The future

Though coal is once again in an ascendant phase there is no guarantee that later political administrations will continue to endorse its major importance to the nation. The period from 1980 onwards will be the crucial time, for from that date national policy on coal's relationship with oil will no longer be determined by considerations of balance of payments and security of supply – at least for a probable twenty-year period – but by longer-term assessments. These will include issues such as the life of reserves of the fossil fuels, coal, gas and oil, with their implications for both fuel and chemical supplies, and the rate at which nuclear energy can be phased in (which is why some of the relevant issues were examined in the previous chapter).

When I saw Mr Roy Mason, an earlier Minister of Power, and asked for his view of the coal industry after 1980, he spoke of possible unpopular decisions with a perspective of a smaller coal industry – small manpower, highly mechanised, highly productive – while the future era would be one allied with nuclear power. Mr Mason is not directly connected with fuel policies, but key decisions in this crucial field are taken by the whole cabinet, not by the departmental minister alone, and Mason's point of view may represent more than an individual opinion in the Cabinet. The official decision of the present Labour government is endorsement of the *Plan for Coal* with targets for the mid-80s of 42 million tons of new capacity backed by a reversal of the previous decline in capital expenditure on major projects. Will this backing continue?

The new nuclear power stations will in due course come into commission – first, presumably, the long-delayed AGR stations, then perhaps the breeder reactor PFR will show results implying that the commercial version (CFR) of 1320 MW should go ahead, and the new direct steam generating (SGHWR) reactors will be commissioned – and it seems possible that coal may once again find itself in danger of sliding over the hump of the next switchback with a diminishing demand from the CEGB. If this should be the trend, the future for coal will rest very heavily on its use in the more convenient converted forms of gas and oil, while over the following decades it gradually takes over the role of the present petrochemical industry (as the oil starts to run dry) in the combined 'coalplexes' that for the moment are distant visions; these combined units have the potential of sharing material and process costs over resultant electricity, heat, refined fuels and chemicals, transforming the economics of the individual processes. Will these issues be examined without prejudice by better techniques than those applied in the ill-fated 1967 Fuel Policy White Paper? So far the auguries are somewhat ambiguous, to judge by the relationships of expenditure on research and development, indicating both a longer-term commitment of officialdom to nuclear energy, and success in persuading government to accept this as policy.

The coal-mining community has passed through several centuries of often very bitter experience, and the industry as a whole has passed through long periods of great difficulty. Now there seem to be real opportunities for winning the fuel in entirely new conditions almost free of blood on the coal and with great personal satisfaction in achievement as the miners become ever more skilled technicians controlling complex machines to extract the valuable mineral from the earth, aided by an increasing array of scientific devices and of scientific method applied to their operations, within a framework of national service. Under nationalisation they work with an administration committed to full consultation and to providing service to the nation as a whole, to the customers and to those engaged in the industry. Certainly for the next decade or so there is a great future for an industry working at high efficiency with high outputs per manshift keeping unit costs low. Beyond this, very much

Fig 12   National Coal Board areas.

depends on a group of factors which must include the cost of coal, its relation to the cost of oil, the relationship between coal-fired and nuclear-powered electricity generation, the successes of research in remotely-controlled mining and in developing economical coal conversion processes; but it may also turn on the prejudices of civil servants guiding their ministers on policies that affect these relationships, and on the political attitudes of our masters at that time.

Will we continue to measure progress in terms of increasing industrial production, and if so will it still necessarily call for an exponential rise in energy consumption? Or will we have started to introduce radical measures to break this relationship and control the soaring demand by conserving and retrieving waste heat, notably from power stations, reducing the need to call on the power within the atom with its consequent potential for grave danger?

For coal, one of our largest indigenous resources, this could be a situation of great promise and great opportunity, despite the handicaps of an extractive industry compounded – in human terms – by the scepticism of the men, and – in physical terms – by past inadequate investment, both due to the period of running down the industry as national policy. Because of this heritage, it is only the nearer future that is at all clear. Everything beyond that will need to be fought for.

Summer 1976

Index